A deeply powerful and resonant piece for the creative soul that lies within.

—**Alexa Meade**, artist

Creative Courage reveals a compelling and original path for our organizations to become more agile and to thrive. Its inspiring and inclusive message calls for our collective work to become highly creative and deeply nurturing. *Creative Courage* is transformative.

—**Susan David**, PhD, author of the #1 *Wall Street Journal* bestseller *Emotional Agility* and psychologist at Harvard Medical School

I've been a student of great innovators, business tycoons, and CEOs for twenty years. By far the most predictive leadership quality is courage, particularly when a bold new path is needed. Taking decisive action in the face of massive uncertainty can be a lonely experience. Vulnerabilities are exposed. Red flags are raised. Yet creativity demands it. Welby's book is an absolute must read for anyone aspiring to make an impact in the business world. You'll not only learn how to be a better leader, you'll be inspired to be a better human being.

—**Jeffrey Cohn**, author of award winning book *Why Are We Bad at Picking Good Leaders* (Jossey Bass), as well as numerous *Harvard Business Review* articles on leadership and innovation

In *Creative Courage*, Welby Altidor deftly expands the scope of what we traditionally call creative practice to include those from all callings and walks of life. Drawing illustrative threads from both the personal and professional, Altidor weaves a vision that is not only inspiring, but also provides the reader tools for moving towards imaginative action. Whether on the world stage or the theater of our own day-to-day lives, *Creative Courage* can help bring freshness and agility to how we approach our collaborations with others.

—**Lucianne M. Walkowicz**, Baruch S. Blumberg NASA Chair of Astrobiology, Library of Congress, astrophysicist at The Adler Planetarium, TED fellow, artist

Creative Courage makes you look at the process of creation in a whole new light! Definitely a book to live by when you want to take your creative and collaborative skills to the next level. Just a great read for inspiring minds."

—**Jon Boogz**, movement artist

When I met Welby Altidor, one of the very first things he asked me was, "What are your dreams?" Welby has the gift of tapping right into your loftiest imagination . . . and simultaneously giving you the sense that you just might achieve it. It's not a wonder. Welby has had backstage access to some of the most incredible creative talent on the planet. Written in a deeply personal and thoughtful voice, this book offers readers a chance to feel a part of Welby's world and find the creative courage they need to pursue their dreams.

—**Deborah Yeh**, senior vice president,
marketing & brand, Sephora Americas

Creative Courage brings a new ideological vocabulary that can spark epiphanies. It reminds us that the experience of creation is as important as the result of the work. After all, the journey of creation is what makes our daily life.

—**Asinnajaq**, curator and filmmaker, *Three Thousand*

This book highlights the power of the collective genius of true 'intuition driven' co-creation. It focuses on a three-way interaction—
1. A man's personal story. 2. A man's professional story. 3. How a man magnificently encapsulates his audience.

If you channel what you genuinely feel from your very essence (not from your past story), your truth will show up in the most unexpected ways. A truly brilliant read.

—**Duncan D. Bruce**, founding partner and
executive creative director, The Brand Conspiracy & Associates ltd;
author of *Brand Enigma* and *The Dream Café*

CREATIVE COURAGE

CREATIVE COURAGE

Leveraging Imagination, Collaboration, and Innovation to Create Success Beyond Your Wildest Dreams

WELBY ALTIDOR

WILEY

Published by John Wiley & Sons, Inc., Hoboken, New Jersey
Published simultaneously in Canada

For general information about our other products and services, please contact our Customer Care Department within the United States at (800) 762-2974, outside the United States at (317) 572-3993 or fax (317) 572-4002.

Wiley publishes in a variety of print and electronic formats and by print-on-demand. Some material included with standard print versions of this book may not be included in e-books or in print-on-demand. If this book refers to media such as a CD or DVD that is not included in the version you purchased, you may download this material at http://booksupport.wiley.com. For more information about Wiley products, visit www.wiley.com.

Library of Congress Cataloging-in-Publication Data
Names: Altidor, Welby, 1973- author.
Title: Creative courage : leveraging imagination, collaboration, and
   innovation to create success beyond your wildest dreams / Welby Altidor.
Description: Hoboken : Wiley, 2017. | Includes bibliographical references and index. |
Identifiers: LCCN 2017020718 (print) | LCCN 2017035043 (ebook) |
   ISBN 9781119347262 (pdf) | ISBN 9781119347644 (epub) | ISBN 9781119347224 (hardback)
Subjects: LCSH: Creative ability in business. | Leadership. | Success in
   business. | Altidor, Welby, 1973- | Cirque du Soleil. | BISAC: BUSINESS &
   ECONOMICS / Careers / Job Hunting. | BUSINESS & ECONOMICS / Human
   Resources & Personnel Management. | BUSINESS & ECONOMICS / Management.
Classification: LCC HD53 (ebook) | LCC HD53 .A428 2017 (print) | DDC
   650.1–dc23
LC record available at https://lccn.loc.gov/2017020718

Printed in the United States of America

10 9 8 7 6 5 4 3 2 1

For Ella Farber Altidor and the sixteen-year-old misfit hiding in all of us.
No one will get your light until you get it.

Kindness

Before you know what kindness really is
you must lose things,
feel the future dissolve in a moment
like salt in a weakened broth.
What you held in your hand,
what you counted and carefully saved,
all this must go so you know
how desolate the landscape can be
between the regions of kindness.
How you ride and ride
thinking the bus will never stop,
the passengers eating maize and chicken
will stare out the window forever.

Before you learn the tender gravity of kindness
you must travel where the Indian in a white poncho
lies dead by the side of the road.
You must see how this could be you,
how he too was someone
who journeyed through the night with plans
and the simple breath that kept him alive.

Before you know kindness as the deepest thing inside,
you must know sorrow as the other deepest thing.
You must wake up with sorrow.
You must speak to it till your voice
catches the thread of all sorrows
and you see the size of the cloth.
Then it is only kindness that makes sense anymore,
only kindness that ties your shoes
and sends you out into the day to gaze at bread,
only kindness that raises its head
from the crowd of the world to say
It is I you have been looking for,
and then goes with you everywhere
like a shadow or a friend.

Naomi Shihab Nye*

* "Kindness" from *Words Under the Words: Selected Poems* by Naomi Shihab Nye, copyright © 1995. Reprinted with the permission of Far Corner Books.

CONTENTS

ACKNOWLEDGMENTS

To Ella, for being the amazing dancer of life. To Kat, for being the visionary of love, space, and pace. To Yael, for being an extraordinary mother and artist. To Annie, Dorcelan, Myrta, and Wendy, for your faith and love. To the Baulu family, for your art of hosting and celebrating. To Susan Abramovitch, for practicing law so artfully. To Jeanenne Ray at Wiley, for your patience and support. To Jocelyn Kwiatkowski, also at Wiley, and your valiant team of editors, thank you for your hawk eyes and for being the guardians of the reading flow. To Adrienne Brodeur from the Aspen Institute, for reminding me to listen to my favorite podcast, *On Being*. To Alissa Nutting, for your sense of time and your generosity in Aspen. To Guy Laliberté, for your business savvy and your creative intelligence. To Danielle Serpica at Wiley, for your rigor and mastery of the process. To my fellow students at Aspen Words, Colorado, for your courage to share that gave me wings. To Michel Rioux, for your love of theater. To the small but mighty team of Aspen Words, for showing me the way. To Jean "Creative Guide at Cirque du Soleil" François Bouchard, for your intuition. To Murielle Cantin, for your supersonic ability to see the potential in others and for seeing the talent seeker in me. To John Branca and Karen Langford of the Michael Jackson Estate, for your intimate knowledge of the art and genius of the king of pop. To Bernard Petiot, for your intellectual agility. To Boris Verkhovsky, for being a precious storyteller. To Fabrice Becker, for the music. To Jamie King, for being punk rock and for sharing its spirit with me. To Carla Kama, for being real and badass. To Matthew Whelan, for the wet towels of truth. To Joel Bergeron, for having our back and helping us to see the stage. To Carole Doucet, for challenging and encouraging me to find the questions inside the questions. To Brian Drader, for connecting words and visions to life on stage. To Joanne Fillion, for encouraging me to aim for just enough

xiv Acknowledgments

perfection. To Line Giasson, for your drive to make auditions memorable. To Diane Quinn, for your fearless embrace of the spirit of the Renaissance. To Bernardine Fontaine, for your strength that inspired me, and our family, to be strong. To Jacques Méthé, for your sense of words and story. To Catherine Nadeau, for your sense of beauty in movement. To Marta Rocamora, for your sense of community. To Viviana De Loera, for your sense of space. To Seth Godin, for Linchpin live in New York City in 2010. To David and Tom Kelly from IDEO, for the creative confidence. To David Allen, for Getting Things Done. To Marche Soupson, for the almost daily stroll to get delicious soup for lunch. To Fabrik8 in Montreal, for the office space. To Stephanie Malak and Emanuel Cohen, for your keen sense of lines and objects, thanks for the graphs and icons in this book. To the MJ ONE team, for your resilience, brilliance, and bigheartedness. To everyone at Cirque du Soleil, your passion makes your audience radiant.

For all of your superpowers and your genius, thank you!

FOREWORD

When I met Welby for the first time, one could say that part of the setting was somewhat familiar to the world I was creating in the script of the TV show *CSI*. There was obscurity surrounding us, even if we were not in a dark alley. Then the shadowy, tensed atmosphere was sporadically disturbed by shots of light and music, video projections, dances, and incredible acrobatics and by a flurry of activities onstage and in the working theater, filled with computers, artists, technicians. As I sat with my team at the back of the house, I felt the whole energy of Las Vegas concentrated inside the performing space where Welby was busy creating the show *Michael Jackson ONE* with Jamie King and a talented team from Cirque du Soleil and beyond.

I grew up in Las Vegas, where my love for music and live stage performances started. My mother worked at the Riviera Hotel, where legends like Bill Withers and the 5th Dimension performed. Music never stopped inspiring me. So, it was extra special for me to meet with Welby at that moment. He was in the middle of creating a hit show, although he didn't know it back then. That too was familiar; I was catching him as the work was still in progress, in flux, in that fragile and vulnerable place where you are not sure if it's going to work or not, your heart full of hope and caffeine.

I should know a thing or two about being vulnerable and about dancing with the unknown. When I first imagined, dreamed, and created the TV show *CSI*, nobody knew about me in Hollywood. As a young guy from Las Vegas, I was representing in many ways the cliché of the misfit with not much more than a dream and a few dollars to his name.

Creating something new that resonates with many is hard. It's never an exact science although the process is always exacting. And at the core of that process lies a subtle, often overlooked question: Can we create something amazing, innovative, without crushing our soul and the spirit of our team in the process? Is it inevitable to do great work at a great cost to you and the team that surrounds you? Is leadership, creative and otherwise, only about sacrifices?

I pitched the idea of a TV script following a team of forensic experts investigating in Las Vegas (and subsequently in New York, Miami, and even the cyber world!) many times before someone said yes. I had to absorb many "NOs!" along the way, uttered at times in the most impersonal way, as body blows coming from left and right. I was lucky to meet through it all talented, visionary, and courageous people who decided to bet on my potential, starting with celebrated producer Jerry Bruckheimer and acclaimed TV executive Nina Tassler.

I love that Welby explores in this book two concepts that are fundamental to my vision of success. Creativity, of course, and courage. As an artist and an outsider in Hollywood back then, I aimed to break the rules by offering a different approach to storytelling on TV that changed the standards and the paradigm of that era. So much so that it inspired a generation of shows that adopted and were inspired by it. That creativity and thirst for innovation are at the heart of what drives my work, whether I dream of new TV series, Broadway shows, or a celebration of cutting-edge diversity through the medium of comic books.

As a producer, I can never take for granted courage, a quality that is critical to lasting and impactful success. It's a mind-set that I have in part acquired thanks to my childhood in Las Vegas, where I learned the value of risk-taking. The risk-taker can be reckless of course, mindless or arrogant, but I prefer the courageous ones who—like some of my mentors—never shy away from taking a chance on the misfits, the odd man or odd woman out. It takes courage to zig when the world zags, but this truism is also at the heart of creativity, innovation, and success.

Since that first day where we met in the theater of the Mandalay Bay hotel in Las Vegas, Welby and I continued to foster a precious friendship, peppered with dreams of collaborating together on projects and mutual support, admiration for our respective work and ethos.

Through the last few years, I've known Welby to be passionate about creating beautiful live experiences and shows with Cirque du Soleil, but I also discovered his passion for improving the way that beauty and innovation is created. Welby's obsession covers not only the output of work but also the process that leads to its creation. Said differently, he's driven to create amazing things amazingly. Fearlessly, he wants to improve not only the "what" but also the "how" of innovation.

I've had the privilege to work with incredible teams of supremely talented showrunners, producers, and actors. I know firsthand how much the quality of our process or lack thereof affects the final product, the story, the result. The way we treat people and the way we find productive ways to work together and harmonize our individual styles and beliefs all contribute to making our shows and our businesses great—or not.

And for every project and each new milestone, that quest needs reinvention through courage, creativity, and humility. In my industry, we are never completely in control of the destiny of our work. We are constantly waiting for a yes, for the green light of someone else on the project on which we are working. Although this is a reality that can't be completely erased or contoured, *Creative Courage: Leveraging Imagination, Collaboration, and Innovation to Create Success Beyond Your Wildest Dreams* invites us beautifully and convincingly to start by saying yes to ourselves and the potential of our dreams.

In that way, Welby's thoughts represent an expression of what I tried to convey years ago when I named my production company Dare to Pass. I invite you to join Welby's vivid explorations and in the process, refuse to pass on your wildest dreams. Whether you are moving on something new, closing a chapter of your life, going deeper into your current practice, or searching for the meaning of your next quest, the stories and insights that you will discover in *Creative Courage* will make a difference for you and your teams. Wherever you are and whatever you do, it will inspire you to write and rewrite your precious story.

Anthony E. Zuiker
Creator and Executive Producer, *CSI*

PREFACE

I believe that a work culture that supports the growth of its employees creates more favorable conditions for its brand, its products, its services to be and stay relevant. Our well-being, our ability to lead efficiently and creatively, is connected to the quality of our culture at work. That culture can suffer from the tension between the status quo and the need for transformation. In fact, in every culture, we find forces aimed at preserving the status quo and opposing energies dedicated to its transformation.

In that potential conflict sits the promise of creativity, innovation, and breakthroughs. Finding the harmony between these two necessary forces is not easy, and when one force takes over too radically or disruptively, the other force likely reacts. When the status quo tries to impose itself resolutely, the war on imagination lives strong, as a state of conflict where imagination, free association of ideas and the connection of unrelated concepts, or diverse teams and people is strongly discouraged, even punished. In other words, when the status quo takes over, the war on imagination follows. When the energy of transformation goes too fast for the people it affects, we are left with incomprehension, anger, and reactionary retraction from the world. We step back into our identities and our politics when at work. I call these moments in organizations, *brand grabs*. We hold on to a less than optimal, often nostalgic vision of who we are.

The distress between status quo and transformation stems from obvious and obscure reasons. The dramatic advances in computing and one of its by-products, quicker, more voluminous disseminations of information, is one factor in the worsening of the dynamic and coupling between what's stable and what's transforming. This situation challenges almost everything in our world, from the way we call a taxi, think about mobility and transportation, to the way that we will consume entertainment in the future.

Consequently, becoming relevant and staying relevant has become harder for organizations and brands. As the newest rapidly replaces the new, the pressure on the bottom line expands, and the need to innovate grows faster while the cycles of discoveries stay practically unchanged. We know that we need to evolve by staying agile and nimble. But we also don't want to lose our identity, our culture, I hear leaders say.

So how can we create or nurture a more innovative culture at work to answer the call of transformation? How can we leverage imagination and creativity to make our work more robust and resilient? And how can such a culture help produce relevance inside and outside our organization? Moreover, and more fundamentally, as we face those challenges, do we have to choose between a high-performance culture that helps generate great value at a very high human cost, or a nurturing culture that sacrifices value, innovation and performance for the integrity of the life inside all of us? De we have to choose between value and values?

I believe that we can bridge the gap between value and values, between high-performance and nurturing space for meaningful work. By learning to lead with creative courage, we can help create a culture for our organization that's more innovative and more able to answer the call of transformation. At its core, the practice of leading with creative courage offers an evolving and open cycle of seven integrated, incremental practices: (1) care first, (2) secure safety, (3) foster trust, (4) play with danger, (5) dream, (6) discover break-throughs, (7) and grow. Under the umbrella of creative courage, these practices that I also refer to as stages or dimensions offer a powerful framework that you can adapt to your reality as you help yourself and your organization transform while staying true to your most important principles. Leading with creative courage offers support on the path to inside-out relevance for you and your organization.

INTRODUCTION

I care, therefore I am; I hope, therefore I am; I imagine, therefore I am. I am ethical, therefore I am. I have a purpose, therefore I am. I pause and reflect, therefore I am.

Dov Seidman[1]

I n traditional theater, when the curtain finally rises, it reveals what was temporarily hidden, unknown, unconscious, and protected from the light. The moments just before the curtain opens are potent: with preparation, vulnerability, doubts, delight, surprises, and hope for relevance. Ideally, after the curtain rises, a mirror-like effect is created between the audience, those who are watching or reading what's revealed, and the performers, those who are revealing their story. Through the beauty and the failures of the characters presented to us, we see our own beauty and failures. In some ways, the light of theater can set us free if it dares to reveal courageous truths. Therefore, from the personal and distinctive details fearlessly shared, something universal emerges. Progressively, we recognize and deeply feel, thanks to that light shining on the truth and the mystery of our lives, something that in the best cases can even inspire us to take action. That process of revelation is at the heart of creativity, imagination, innovation, and telling stories. Even before we had curtains to reveal our stories, we had the open stage of the circus and of ancient Rome's Colosseum, for example. And before that, we simply gathered in a circle, with a fire in the middle as our light.

.t and Present Clash

Do you know what Michael Jackson, Marilyn Monroe, Frida Kahlo, Nelson Mandela, Plato, Muhammad Yunus, and Bob Dylan have in common? They all challenged the status quo of their time in periods that felt transformational and unprecedented. By questioning how music or race was strictly segregated, how women were supposed to relate to their sensuality or identity in public, what corrupted youth, what folk music was supposed to be, or how banks operated, these icons clashed with the past in a way that made them relevant and memorable to us. In fact, in every culture through time, there have been forces aimed at preserving the status quo and opposing energies dedicated to its transformation.

For close to sixteen years, I worked at Cirque du Soleil, arguably one of the world's most influential and important live entertainment companies in our time. I became then a passionate member of a unique, stimulating, and challenging work culture, and I eventually played one of the leading roles in the creative destiny of the organization. I learned to work at an exceptionally fast pace. On one side, I could see in full bloom the beauty of creativity, imagination, and the fearless drive to innovate. And on the other side, I witnessed and benefited from the powerful leverage of business savvy and commerce at play.

Cirque du Soleil contributed to reinventing the circus by marrying industry and artistry, theater and sports, creativity and commerce, individual imagination and the strengths of the collective. Cirque rose as a challenger to the traditional understanding of what a circus could and couldn't be and in this way brought an unexpected modernity to an ancient form. Creativity, imagination, and innovation find their most vivid expression at the center of that same tension between the past and the present.

The Uncertainty of Transformation

In periods of profound transformation, that tension between past and present is highly volatile, and it can increase to the point that it challenges the coexistence of our heritage, our current situation, and our aspirations to transform the present. This increasing tension affects our world today and, by extension, our lives and our work. In such times, uncertainty expands, and as a response, the urgency for finding new solutions to complex problems increases as well. It's a dynamic driving us to innovate, transform, adapt, and even ride change to prevent being a victim of unpredictable, blind transformations. This pressure to innovate and renew ourselves while honoring our past creates fear, confusion, and doubts. And when we fall in the crack of that tension, between past and present, we can easily feel that we are misfits, like teenagers awkwardly standing between two ages.

Under that pressure, we might ask ourselves if we are going in the right direction at work. We might wonder how we keep up with the volume and the speed of changes in our life and the lives of those around us. We wonder: Are we safe? Will robots replace us? Are we about to be outsourced, outmaneuvered, or shipped away?

Looking to find solutions, we might also wonder how we can create or nurture a more innovative culture at work to answer the call of transformation. How can we leverage imagination and creativity to make our work and our organizations more robust and resilient? And how can such a culture help produce relevance both inside and outside our organization?

Around the world, start-ups, corporations, teams, dance troupes, board members, co-working space leaders, community organizations, political groups, companies, and, yes, circus collectives, also ask how can they create or foster more positive, constructive working environments. They discuss how the cultures created at work can be not only productive but nurturing, resilient, and supportive of growth, transformation, and innovation.

In my work with leaders from industries as diverse as technology, banking, beauty care, sports apparel, architecture, and design, all the way to the world of creativity in entertainment, and live experience, which I know the most, those questions arise in different shapes and forms. Visionary leaders from all walks of life and with very different focuses wonder how to integrate more innovation and creativity in the work that they do and ask how this can be done in a way that brings more value to their group:

- How do we deliver relevance, meaning something that truly matters, to the people that we serve?
- How do we build businesses that have a long-term and sustainable, positive impact on the world?

- How do we stay relevant considering our past successes?
- How do we work better together?
- How do we draw the best from our teams?
- How do we make the best of our projects?
- How do we create a lasting, positive, constructive impact on the people we serve and on the world?

These simple, yet provocative, difficult questions and the discussions they lead to have inspired me to reflect on my twenty-year experience in the entertainment world. In this book, although I honor the rich, unavoidable influence that Cirque du Soleil has had on my thinking, I speak in my own name rather than in the name of Cirque. Nonetheless, I also refer to my journey within this exceptional company that has provided so much inspiration for my career.

Making Sense of My Experience

As a passionate creator and observer of the world of entertainment, but also the world of work, art, management, leadership, and creativity, I saw an opportunity to share my understanding, my point of view, and my vision in this book. No one can answer these questions alone, and there is no one answer for everyone. But these important questions draw out different contributions and points of view to help answer the call of our transforming world. Beyond answers, they also lead to more questions that might be a source of inspiration for your own work and your transformation. I believe that our well-being, our ability to innovate, to lead efficiently and creatively, is connected to the quality of our culture at work. Moreover, I believe that a work culture that supports the growth of its employees and members creates favorable conditions for its brand to be and stay relevant and profitable.

As I started to gain perspective on my professional practice and what made a positive difference in my work over time, I began to see the main source of my successes and the deeper understanding of my failures through a mind-set that I call *creative courage*. I believe that the underpinnings behind and the practice of creative courage can help transform the way we work and engage the questions most of us ask about work and innovation.

What Is Creative Courage?

I draw inspiration from different definitions and from my personal practice to define in my own words what *creativity* and *courage* mean:

1. *Creativity:* Leveraging original ideas or unrelated ideas or remixing ideas to produce something artful, skillful, or masterful that questions, persuades, or moves. It's imagination writing a sentence with an invented grammar. Creativity is not limited to art; rather, being alive itself is being potentially creative, and so it is an expression of life.

2. *Courage:* Deciding to move forward toward the unknown, the uncertain or the certain, despite being afraid.

Small children often have an advantage over adults when it comes to being able to practice creative courage because they are still in touch with their "explorer of the unknown" side. They constantly invent new solutions to tough problems, and since they can't read yet, instruction booklets are pointless.

Developing the mind-set of creative courage when things were hard at work gave me confidence professionally. I was influenced by a set of values and experiences like grit, confidence, perseverance, relentlessness, compassion, a sense of survival, desperation, discouragement, crippling doubts, detachment, and resilience. These words form a background behind my thinking about creative courage and its practice.

Practicing creative courage means developing a mental posture that helps us move forward in the world, despite a fear of rejection and failure. It suggests that we can work with the objective of bringing value to ourselves and others. Our goal when we practice creative courage is to provoke important questions, offer valuable answers, support insight, and see every emotion as noble.

It suggests a graceful movement forward, knowing that we can always improve our ability to be more in touch with our skillfulness. It proposes a path to develop our ability to share our creative courage with others. And it offers an open door to embrace what's artful in us. We can find the paths in us that point toward mastery and even virtuosity, no matter who we are and what we do. Practicing creative courage proposes routes to move past the fear of failure. There we find a new path toward the joy of bringing something essential to our life and that of others. In concrete terms, it means learning to passionately love discovering through the unknown. It means facing head-on a difficult challenge, a problem that at the moment seems impossible to resolve, even embracing a situation where most would doubt you or your group could succeed.

Relevance becomes the ultimate currency, a new, unconventional factor that I like to call our *high line*–expanding our conventional pre-occupations for the bottom line of our organization. So I argue here that beyond the traditional thinking we have about profit and balance sheet (*bottom line*), we must integrate in our aspiration a high line thinking about relevance, meaning, and resonance for the people that we create for and that ultimately benefit from our work.

Finally, creative courage refers to that voice inside you that moves past the accusatory, contemptuous whisper, "Who do you think you are?" and tries to create something beautiful nonetheless or something meaningful, even if the risk of rejection or failure is great. Simply saying "Forward, nonetheless, forward despite it all, forward despite the fear" triggers a momentum of its own and builds inside you a mind-set that can transform the way you lead your life, the teams you support, the projects you craft, and the organizations that you belong to. As a mind-set, it changes our perspective on solving unusual and unconventional problems. It makes us accept and embrace the fact that many of our relevant and crucial challenges have no instruction booklet. It refers to an inner game of creativity, a mentality to be developed over time yet instantly accessible. It is not only a set of techniques and tips. It suggests that at the heart of management, leadership, and business, there is a profound call and a yearning for an approach that's artful, heart-full, and truly supports creativity, innovation, and growth.

Although the practice of creative courage and the mind-set behind it can help us find solutions to tough, nearly impossible problems to solve, the more potent power of creative courage can help us make sense of our differences, transforming them into a powerful advantage for business, leadership, and innovation. It can trigger a belief in our ability to find solutions to problems despite the absence of an instruction manual or ready-made answers. Practicing our leadership with the framework it proposes can support our efforts to bridge the gap over our complex diversity, leveraging our imagination to find the gold in what makes us disparate yet connected.

In this way, we can dramatically improve our skills at integrating diverse groups of people (diverse in terms of age, gender, talents, abilities, geography, backgrounds, disciplines, beliefs, and aspirations, for example) in the context of dissimilar and complex sets of challenges. We end up growing when we tackle projects that can influence the world positively in small and big ways. Practicing creative courage means calling for a new form of artistry at work—an artistry that's asking us to integrate elements, knowledge, and practices that we already know to help do visionary work. Finally, this practice will inspire us to integrate the past and the present of our business and work more constructively than we've done previously.

No Panacea

From my work as a casting agent for films and TV projects, all the way to working with some of the world's most talented artists, performers, businesses, and production professionals, I've seen, observed, lived, and had the privilege to work through the exhilaration of leading with creative courage. I have also witnessed and suffered from the perils of being disconnected from my creative courage.

Despite its promises, creative courage is not a panacea. You don't necessarily need constructive values and work practices like inclusion, collaboration, and creativity to make things happen or to create value through innovation. You can give orders to people, work in silos, in secrecy even, forcing those around you to execute on your vision without building from their input or taking their aspirations into account. The sad truth is that you can enslave people and still find a way to create value by exploiting them. Yet, it is common knowledge (if not common practice) that many progressive human resources leaders around the world now recognize or advise their CEOs, presidents, and boards to find ways to "engage," empower their employees and every member of their groups to build organizations that support everyone's growth rather than just the growth of the business or a happy few. Most of us want to work in an organization that offers us as much as we offer the organization, whether it belongs to us or to someone else. I believe that we all want to thrive.

The Quest for a Constructive, Transformative Workplace

How can we create a workplace that's empowering, inclusive, and a source of breakthrough innovation? How can the necessary drive of a company for its own growth find harmony with the evolution of its employees, team members, and collaborators? To grow, to win, do we have to choose between innovative performance and human well-being? All over the world, people of all ages, sectors, ranks, and aspirations are asking themselves the same question.

Creative courage attempts to advance the discussion behind these questions by providing inspiration on your journey and asking questions that you can carry with you beyond the confine of these pages. How can we bring the bottom line and the high line together? How can we create organizations that remain and become relevant inside and out? That yearning translates into our ability to lead change that improves our world. Creative courage aims at inspiring rather than simply prescribing, because every difficult and complex situation requires creativity and imagination.

Creative Courage for Everyone

I've said earlier that I believe that we all yearn to thrive and grow at work individually and collectively, no matter who we are or what age we have reached. We can join great companies, create and lead distinctive organizations, or work on projects of our own design that we are passionate about.

My invitation to you, in this book, is to join me and see how improving your organization's innovation culture means improving its entire culture. If you separate or enclose the innovation units, that is like putting creativity in a corner of your company, missing the opportunity to expand the mind-set of creative courage to everyone inside of your group. There is a collective opportunity for everyone in your organization to integrate the mind-set of creativity, imagination, and innovation and to contribute to the present and future relevance of your projects, goals, and aspirations. The days when only a few people in your organization had the monopoly on innovation are either numbered or already a thing of the past. In that spirit, I've develop a framework, inspired by my personal professional practice, that I hope is simple without being simplistic, and that extends on the mind-set of creative courage.

As you will discover, this framework can help create or consolidate your personal and organizational innovation culture. It can also help you to practice even stronger strategic review of your innovation culture at any level of your company or other type of organization. Whether you're a CEO or start-up entrepreneur, the framework underneath creative courage can help you assess your best practices, identify the area where something is missing or needs to improve, eliminate the approaches that are counter-productive to your innovation culture, and find the creativity to invent new practices when needed.

My hope is that *Creative Courage* inspires you and people everywhere—in government, business, organizations big or small, mature companies and starts-ups, and, of course, the professional creative world. We all can use creative courage to make our projects and businesses better. The practices that I discuss are not exhaustive or all original to me, but I've used all of them, and my hope is that you do too, challenging them, improving them, and adding some of your own imagination.

As I wrote this book, I was reminded of how important a role humility can play when we tackle enormous challenges. Creativity, imagination, and innovation are messy, and through creative courage, we can find beauty in that too. We can discover what a colleague at Cirque inspired me to integrate years ago: things are not perfect, but we can strive for just enough *perfection*, what she called "perfect enough." As a repented perfectionist, I discovered that in the process of creating something beautiful, impactful, and meaningful, I could settle for more than just *good enough* without getting cut in the elusive quest for perfection, was also an inspiration to the practice of creative courage.

Each of the following chapters has three main sections that will be identified by their respective icons: section I (⌒) raises the curtain on a personal story, often close to me, focusing on the narrative elements relevant to the main theme chapter; section II (⌒), titled *Insights*, explores concepts, practical applications, and questions that you might find useful to continue your reflection; and section III (◉), *Your Story*, offers a space for your own reflection, reaction, and emotions to the content to expand. In this section I also summarize the essence of the chapter and add a checklist of few key reminders.

I encourage you to take many notes as you read and see your reading more as the beginning of a discussion rather than as commandments. I try to approach the theme of this book from a personal standpoint, borrowing at some times the style of a memoir and at others a creative playbook. Always, my intention has been to approach things as simply as possible, again while avoiding being simplistic. In my work onstage and beyond, I aim for profound simplicity, no matter the subject. It's my way to attempt at speaking truth.

I begin this exploration of the practice of creative courage by looking first at what makes any culture–at work and beyond–compelled to discourage imagination, what I call the *war on imagination*. To better understand the scope of what practicing creative courage means, it's relevant to better understand what happens when we live through a culture that discourages or makes it difficult to be creatively courageous. Even more so, it's pertinent to see what can happen when we integrate the rules of that culture, the war on imagination, in us. In fact, I can say that I discovered my creative courage, in large part, after losing it.

CHAPTER 1

The Central Problem Affecting Work

The War on Imagination, and How I Lost My Creative Courage

Have cake and tea with your demons. When we shun our own darkness (our weaknesses, our anger, our sadness, our shame, our pain), we are disconnecting ourselves from the full spectrum of elements that exists within ourselves and the rest of the universe.

Yumi Sakugawa[1]

I. Raising the Curtain

Finding in North Korea the Words for an Old Problem

I was on my way to lunch in Pyongyang, the capital of North Korea, officially the Democratic Republic of Korea (DPRK), on my third day there. Every day at the Koryo Hotel, one of the only lodging options in the city for foreigners, I was greeted by an ageless man as the elevator's doors opened. His responsibilities seem to be to discreetly smile when someone entered the elevator and press the buttons leading to the appropriate floors. From my limited point of view, his third task seemed the most consequential. It was to arrange, impeccably, a doormat-size carpet on the elevator's floor indicating, in English, the day of the week. The daily ritual of leaving my room and walking through an absurdly dimly lit corridor on one of the highest floors of the hotel was systematically accompanied by this visual reference to the current day of the week. Monday, Tuesday, Wednesday . . . And it was on that Wednesday that I was about to feel a visceral and sudden unease and fear when I discovered a four-headed monster that was hiding in plain sight.

My temperature rose, I felt disoriented, panicked. The monster was invisible yet powerful. On one head, I could suddenly see its dysfunction and on another one how it was a result of a profound clash between the past and the present. The third head turned at various speeds, abnormally, unusually. The last head, the fourth one, appeared completely disconnected, from the other ones, unaware.

Why I Was in North Korea

Some of the world's best flying trapeze acts ever created come mostly from the former Soviet Union's countries (Russia, Ukraine), from China, and, less known, from North Korea. For close to two decades, troupes from North Korea won many major prizes and gold medals in some of the most prestigious festivals and competitions on the international circus arts event circuit: Monte Carlo, Monaco, Circus of Tomorrow in Paris, Zhuhai in China, and others. In fact, they typically won the biggest prize in their category.

The reputation of these troupes in the international talent scouting circles was not a secret, and everyone also knew that it was nearly impossible to hire artist troupes from that region other than for short stints in international festivals and performances in China. The prestige of those flying trapeze troupes was a source of pride for North Korea and its government was actively supporting their development. Circus in North Korea was an outlet to demonstrate the talent of its designers in acrobatics and the might of its people. Bringing such a troupe to the Cirque du Soleil, based in the West, and offering contracts spanning generally two years suggested major, controversial, cultural clashes. In short, it felt impossible to bring such a troupe to the West despite their recognized talents.

A New Role for Me: Cultural Diplomat

I was in North Korea by mere chance. By the beginning of 2008, I had already played several important functions at Cirque du Soleil within the talent casting team. I had traveled the world to find distinctive contortionists and trapeze artists, but also dancers, singers, physical actors, musicians, and even comic actors or clowns who formed the different troupes of the Cirque du Soleil shows. I was now in charge of leading discussions to create collaborations with sports federations, arts organizations, and circus schools around the world. In the evolution of my roles as talent scout and later as director of the casting advising team, I was acting as a sort of cultural diplomat for Cirque du Soleil with the title of strategic relationship director for arts, sports, and circus.

With the company presenting over fifteen different shows simultaneously around the world, my new objective was to facilitate the access and the long-term recruitment of artists by developing an international network of partnerships between Cirque du Soleil and many national and global federations and schools. This role offered me the opportunity to work closely with several pioneers and experts in body movement, entertainment technology, the performing arts, sports high performance, and circus arts at Cirque du Soleil and beyond.

A Beautiful-Impossible Objective

The utopian and positive spirit present in Cirque du Soleil's creation was both a source of inspiration and a reinforcement of some of my instincts. In my naive, idealistic view of the world and my excitement over this new role, I had set a few key goals for myself and the small team I was working with. One of my objectives was to establish the groundwork for an eventual connection between our team of professional acrobatic designers, arguably some of the best in the world, and their counterparts from the Pyongyang National Circus in North Korea. I was dreaming that we could rise beyond the politics of our respective regions, that we could create a cultural bridge to exchange ideas on best practices and innovation in trapeze act design and performances—if or when the situation ever improved between our countries, some time, in an unforeseen, distant future. It was a long shot, what I called a *beautiful-impossible dream*, and what Team X from Google calls Moonshot projects and goals, an objective that I liked to set for myself among more pragmatic milestones.

Whenever I establish a direction for my work and think about its eventual impact, setting at least one truly out-of-the-ordinary objective on my list became a must and a best practice after the experience in North Korea. The founder of Cirque du Soleil, Guy Laliberté, referred at times to the mission of the company as bringing dreams and peace to the world through shows and entertainment, something I translated and adapted as being a warrior for peace and dreams into my work. Inspired by this beautiful-impossible objective and the idea of being a warrior for peace and dreams, I imagine my work to have a potential impact on the horizon of five to seven years. I thought that if I could establish a few critical, strategic contacts in North Korea, even if I was long gone or had moved to a new role at Cirque du Soleil, the casting team would be able to take advantage of that groundwork and eventually create the knowledge and cultural exchange I was visualizing. No one truly believed that this initiative would go anywhere, and so nobody tried to stop me.

Dreams of Peace

I was also considering this project because when I was a child, I had dreamed of becoming a diplomat, helping to achieve peace in the most conflicted parts of our world. Later, at twenty years old, I got emotional when President Bill Clinton invited Prime Minister Yitzhak Rabin and Palestine Liberation Organization chairman Yasser Arafat to "shake hands for peace in the world" at the White House in 1993.

After a short and inconclusive stint in political science at the University of Montreal, Canada, I was left feeling ambivalent about the discipline, while still passionately interested in discovering the inner workings of our world and its potential for peace and harmony. I thought that opening the possibility for our designers and those in North Korea meeting and exchanging innovative ideas on how to make people fly was a way to express a form of creativity. It could move us closer to an inner aspiration for mutual understanding, meaningful insight, and the discovery that art calls for again and again: that beyond our differences, we share something elemental and universal that can unite us all.

There was this possible promise stemming from the fact that anywhere in the world, kids of any origin, background, and culture resonated with awe and wonder when seeing a human fly from one trapeze to another. In something as simple yet as extraordinarily complex as a flying trapeze act, cultures could be transcended, even if just for a moment. In some ways, my idealism and naiveté prevented me from seeing the obvious obstacles; instead they gave me a push to move forward where others might not have even started.

Circus Diplomacy

I reached out to the Canadian embassy in Ottawa in winter and spring 2008, explaining the essence of the project and my role at Cirque du Soleil. I didn't know when I called that the Canadian Foreign Affairs Services was involved, through its embassy in Seoul, South Korea, in quiet efforts to ease the tensions in the region and help engage the North Korean government in international talks toward peace. Just before my call to Ottawa, apparently a new initiative was about to be deployed for engaging with the leadership of North Korea through cultural and social exchanges and discussions. Very quickly after one of my calls with the Canadian diplomatic team in Ottawa and Seoul, a new expression was born: circus diplomacy.

Approximately four months from my first call in Ottawa, I had established a link with North Korea's permanent mission to the United Nation; hosted them in Montreal for a dinner and a tour of our facilities at Cirque du Soleil's International Headquarters; and explained the possibility of eventual cultural exchange between our respective heads of acrobatic design. Where I imagined an outcome over five to seven years, I found myself suddenly catapulted into the middle of diplomatic complexities, nuances, and potential perils of international politics in one of the world's most sensitive and volatile regions.

Even if Cirque du Soleil shows had never made it to North Korea, the designers of the National Circus of Pyongyang, the Ministry of Culture and Foreign Services Department were very aware of Cirque's work and interested in engaging with its representatives. I have no doubt that Cirque's reputation made the process to visit their country, famously difficult to access, not only possible but fast-tracked.

I was accompanied by a colleague from the casting team, an acrobatic talent scout, and the Canadian ambassador to North Korea, based in Seoul, and his retinue, on our way from Beijing to Pyongyang. Arriving at the Pyongyang International Airport was a notable experience. As soon as we crossed the gate at the border, an agent asked for our passports and our cell phones. Each of our phones was placed in an individual burgundy velvet sachet, and kept at the airport during our entire stay.

A Monster at Lunch

In the elevator that Wednesday afternoon at the hotel, three days into this trip, I looked down at the doormat-size carpet and read "WEDNESDAY" in bright yellow, surrounded by a cheerful blue background and a corresponding rectangular yellow lining.

I was making my way to the one functioning revolving restaurant of the two rotating eateries perched near the top of the hotel and offering a prized panoramic view of the city. Although the hotel's capacity was five hundred guests, I estimated that we were probably only fifteen to twenty clients for a staff of about ninety. Through the restaurant's speakers, the persistent music of the revolution echoed, both epic and mysterious, just above the sound of a whisper, as my colleague and I spoke with our guardian who was assigned to follow and lead us everywhere except in our bedroom.

Over cold noodles, a delicious North Korean specialty that can also be served spicy hot, barbecue beef, and a local version of *cheongju*, a fermented clear rice wine similar to Japanese sake, my colleague and I carried on a conversation with our guardian as we would with any other lunch companion. We tried to balance our curiosity to know more about this seemingly impenetrable world we had managed to enter with the invisible boundaries set out by our dissimilar conditions. I knew not to comment on anything political; not to take photographs of political leaders' statues or billboards without authorization; and not to be intrusive about any topics that could be interpreted incorrectly. Despite all that, we shared moments of genuine laughter and could relate to our shared humanity. My initial difficulty with manipulating my plate of brown, slightly translucent cold noodles provided lots of comic relief.

Suddenly the restaurant started revolving, and it offered an astounding view of the city and its blunt, stark attributes. On the horizon was a surreal sight, unthinkable in the West, absent any publicity other than billboards with images of the political leaders of the dynastic Kim family (called "Dear Leaders") or posters glorifying the state's hegemony and power. There were no personal cars in the streets and only scattered working traffic lights; only governmental vehicles were authorized to circulate. The few citizens walking, even without carrying a single bag with them, seemed to carry something indiscernible yet unusually heavy inside them. Through the large windows, I could see a huge chimney in the city center spewing thick gray-white smoke into an increasingly cloudy sky.

The pace of life in the streets of the capital appeared so slow, covert, and halting that I had the vivid impression that everything around me was turning into black and white, not like Madonna's "Vogue" video of 1990 but Chaplin's *Modern Times*. I was suddenly feeling the full force of being a cog in an impersonal, immaterial, and strange machine.

Panic

This was the moment in my trip to North Korea where I unexpectedly became utterly depressed and confused, although there was nothing visible to explain it. Fighting nausea and something akin to an inner panic attack, scared perhaps that I wouldn't be able to leave the country through some terrible, arbitrary misunderstanding, I couldn't shake the feeling that the monotonous procession of weekday doormats, diligently set up in the elevator, would never end.

While I was feeling lost, pessimistic, and struggling to smile, even to my colleague and our keeper, I needed to escape to the bathroom from a city that was bare, austere, and implacable. After days of visiting historical monuments, I couldn't help but notice the broken city lights, exposed in plain sight as a forgotten priority from a time long past. I couldn't pretend not to take stock of the unfinished buildings that once were the promise of the city's aspirational modernity, independence, and pride. I was now the startled witness of a city, a country perhaps, put on pause from a TV remote made in the 1970s, with crumbling buildings and shivering from the cold and the not-so-secret energy crisis.

Staying too long anywhere becomes suspicious, so I quickly used warm water and then a paper cloth to wipe my face dry. I compare my sensation then to being suddenly hit by freezing rain, cold winds, without having an umbrella for protection despite the urgent need to run home.

In Pyongyang, the deep sadness that fell on me and that I had observed in the streets expanded as I sat down and quickly drank a few sips of rice wine with my lunch companions. Disoriented, I was trying not to follow the curved windows of the revolving restaurant. The room's speakers projected the sound of a choir celebrating the valor of North Korea's army. Outside, erected to honor North Korea's official ideology of self-reliance, called *Juche*, stood the country's highest construction: a 560-foot tower with a monumental plastic orange and red flame-shaped light bulb. At night, it was one of the few buildings still lit through the deep darkness of this urban area.

A Beam of Insight with Words

As I had been making my way back to our table while the light was resolutely leaving the cityscape, I was having trouble finding the words for what I was feeling. All of a sudden, a beam of insight revealed a clarity that continues to support my reflections and thinking around creativity and leadership practices. Whether I'm considering how to best mobilize teams, how to support the creation of great cultures, and how to stay relevant to employees, team members, audiences, customers, and clients alike, I owe a lot of inspiration to that moment of disorientation and subsequent discernment. I was able, for the first time in the heart of Pyongyang, to move beyond the emotional intensity of the moment and put personal words on a distinct experience.

I was experiencing in North Korea at that moment the consequences of a phenomenon that I eventually called the *war on imagination*. Following this trip, I tried to understand, articulate, and characterize the attributes of that unique war, as my experience in North Korea led me to observe its pervasiveness, shape-shifting qualities, and core invisibility.

You can recognize the presence of the war on imagination not by the war itself but by its impact (like my physical sensations in North Korea), the conditions that lead to its expansion, and the toxic environment it produces.

In that moment, at my lunch table in the hotel, I felt the overbearing weight of restrictions put on me and my fellow humans in North Korea, and it almost instantly took my breath away. Those who live under that war on imagination ask for permission, authorization, validation, approval, and consent before they do anything, or they just shut down into not asking much from life anymore. Imagination becomes something suspicious and subversive that must be suppressed. Progressively, without realizing it, we bury the truth of who we are and try to hide as best as we can our attraction for the light in life. In its most extreme form, the war on imagination makes you lose sight of the sacredness of any life, including your own.

We typically associate imagination with artistic creativity or technological innovation, but it is a critical mind-set that can influence every aspect of our lives. Imagination represents the potential that we all have to expand on our abilities to use our hearts and minds in visualizing our lives differently from how they currently are. With practice, imagination gives us the power to project mental images of the future that exist only in our mind onto the screen of the present, like in a movie theater. The more we use our heart and mind to project invented realities or parts of made-up realities in our present, the better we become at using the critical skill of imagination. The more we trust our ability to imagine what's not there yet, the better we improve as innovators; integrators of differences, diversities, and possibility makers; and problem solvers. We embrace the dance with the unknown and the chance for us to become sense maker or meaning maker.

Imagination encapsulates our ability to invent the totality or parts of our lives, even if these parts don't exist yet. Finally, imagination can be a source of growth and mental flexibility, beyond the creation of symbols (art), the invention of tools (technology), and the adaptation of languages (coding), for our hearts and minds. Simply put, through imagination, we can dramatically enhance our relationship with life and the life of those around us. The war on imagination threatens all of that.

A Four-Headed Monster

After the pain and subsequent awakening I experienced in North Korea, I started to identify the most fundamental features of the war on imagination and settled on four of them: dysfunctional leadership, a clash between the past and the present, speed anomaly, and deliberate unawareness.

Dysfunctional Leadership

Dysfunctional leadership refers to autocratic-despotic-dogmatic (*I can only be right*), ungenerous (*it's about me, not about you*), or myopic (*all eyes on the bottom line, by any means*) approaches (or combinations of these) to leadership. Usually these destructive leadership attributes are the result of fear, conscious or not, layered on a sophisticated defense or attack mechanism—or both. These leadership approaches are often expressed through hubris (extreme arrogance), insularity, and delusional self-reliance. Certainly my experience in North Korea exposed the extreme of that dysfunction and how logic can become absurd. The entire contents of the hotel bookshop, for example, had more than a thousand books, all authored by North Korea's leaders. The war on imagination is present when the space for dissension, criticism, or opposition to a situation that anyone inside the country would see as unfair is absent.

Clash between the Past and the Present

The clash between the past and the present stems from an aggravated tension between the establishment's values and the transformative power of aspirations anchored in the present. In such an environment, the future is even more unpredictable, blurry, and opaque. Pyongyang then offered an almost physical representation of a city caught between the past and the present. It gave the impression that it tried to physically stop the progression of time, bare-handed. Its core philosophy of self-reliance metamorphosed into extreme protectionism and isolation from most of the rest of the world.

Speed Anomaly

In a context of speed anomaly, things are either moving too slowly or too fast for comfort and clarity. When the pace of needed improvements is too slow for comfort and yearned changes seem almost impossible, a sense of entropy, deterioration, even the absence of movement, can set in. This situation can bring a feeling of backward movement where time traveling becomes a fantasy and opposition to progress becomes the only celebrated development. In this way, we try to hold on to the fleeting past and keep it safe in a box. In contrast, the speed of change and transformation can be so fast that people feel that there's no reasonable time to think and absorb what those revolutions truly represent for their lives.

In speed anomaly, the feeling of being out of touch, of being unable to keep up with the present, is magnified and even exaggerated. Typically, when the values of the past have the upper hand (conservation), the march of transformation slows, and when the present's aspirations take over blindly (transformation), it throws away the references from the past, brusquely, as fast as possible.

As I was driven through Pyongyang and observed the citizens walking to work or home, I'd had the vivid impression of hundreds of thousands of people walking hurriedly, but paradoxically in slow motion, on thousands of treadmills, neither advancing nor going backward. Without being able to explain it, I also felt that this paradox was not exclusive to North Korea.

Deliberate Unawareness

In deliberate unawareness, we put on a blindfold when we face issues and problems that we want to avoid even though we know that they are in front of us. We hope that by ignoring them or even pretending that they are not there, we will be able to thrive without dealing with them. Even when faced with the most obvious evidence, we refuse to see what's in front of us. Everywhere in Pyongyang, there were traces of unfinished projects and the brutal impact left by the passage of time. Construction of the 105-story Ryugyong Hotel, started in 1987, has never been finished. When visitors ask about the immense construction in the middle of the city, their keepers explain that it will be finished very soon.

The Two Pillars of the War on Imagination: Unconsciousness and Time

The war on imagination finds its bedrock in two pillars: unconsciousness and time. Unconsciousness refers to an insular, autocratic, or ungenerous leadership that favors not generosity but control and the fear of losing it as the ultimate currency and source of power. It also encompasses the deliberate and systematic denial of truth or facts that are unwelcome or would put a predetermined course of action in question.

The second pillar, time, refers to the aggravated disharmony between the values from the past and the movement of transformation or innovation in the present. There's always a natural tension between our conventions—the result of our history—on one hand, and our aspirations to improve and grow, on the other hand. The tension between the past and the present, where our imagination thrives, is one of the most profound sources of our creativity and the bridge that allows us to shape the future. These movements forward are supported by discoveries in the world and within ourselves. When this natural tension between these two poles moves beyond a tolerable point, creativity and growth are still possible, but the risk of damaging conflicts, confusion in direction, and destruction also increases.

When that tension is exacerbated, when the cultural anchors grown and established out of heritage clash with the call of transformation and the plea of the future, the profound and dangerous disharmony that emerges contributes to the intensity of the war on imagination. This is usually when we start dreaming of going back in time (*We had so much fun when we were only sixty employees!*), stopping time, or beaming ourselves into the future. In short, when the past and the future fight in the present because of a marked acceleration of changes (technology leap, major historical updates, political change of paradigm, restructuration at work), our ability to use imagination through the filters of our heart and mind is at risk of succumbing to the war.

When we try to make an initial assessment of our culture at work, we might notice an autocratic, insular, or ungenerous leadership at the upper echelon. This is a clear indicator that a war on imagination is brewing. We might also participate in the debate that most organizations will have to grapple with at some point: how to find harmony between their heritage (even start-ups deal earlier than they realize with their culture) and their need to stay relevant in the present and the future.

The easiest, most predictable posture for me in North Korea would be to stand tall, victorious, superior and to say that this was the only place—mysterious, opaque, insular, dictatorial, obstinate, arbitrary, even cruel—where my painful epiphany and such an invisible war could exist and take place. But I realized that what I found in Pyongyang were only the words to describe something I had experienced before. This wasn't the first time that I could sense that my ability to imagine the world could potentially be threatened, challenged, discouraged, even denigrated, in an instant. The more profound insight was that I didn't need to visit Pyongyang to observe in and around me the impact of the war on imagination. That understanding led me to realize that none of us is immune to the presence and the effect of the war on imagination, no matter where we live. At least I now had the words, acting like a spotlight in theater, to call its bluff.

The War Closer to Us

The war on imagination is vicious and pernicious and it doesn't need any political affiliations to rear its four heads. We feel it every time we don't face up to mistakes, discern the sharpness of our limitations, and debunk our delusions. It's there when we become self-righteous, thinking that we have all the answers and consider it more important to be right than happy. It can also do a lot of damage when our inner voice of critic expresses its doubt about our initiatives, our aspirations, and who we truly are. The war on imagination creates a context where we can become rigid, manipulative, arrogant, self-defeating, insular, and even cruel to others and ourselves. When spread inside an entire organization, these attributes expand, affecting the very engagement of its members. It's a war that affects our ability to see the world with love when we are the ones waging it. It guards us against saying "sorry" when we hurt others.

Alternatively, when we fall victim to its aggression, it prevents us from walking in the world with confidence. Impulsively and fearfully, we find ourselves asking for permission just to breathe and exist. And a question we ask ourselves and receive from the world lingers incessantly: "Who do you think you are?"

In both cases, aggressor or victim, the war on imagination promotes an anticreative life, or a creativity channeled toward destruction, subjugation, concrete or metaphoric, of what is not us, of what doesn't look like us, and of what doesn't agree with us. As I observed it in North Korea, the paradox about the extreme form of the war on imagination there was that it could take the life out of you without necessarily killing you, which made it that much more dangerous and insidious.

* * *

In the end, I didn't manage to bring our acrobatic design experts together with theirs and bring about world peace. Flying trapezes didn't stop the tension between humans in the region. Nonetheless, I learned something precious about myself during that trip that I brought all the way back home.

Childhood Dreams and the Personal War

My parents loved me passionately, if not adroitly. They were constantly fearful that something bad would happen to me so they protected my every move. Eventually their control over my young, free-spirited self quickly grew to an intolerable point of no return. According to their filtered view of the world, I couldn't learn to swim with my schoolmates because the indifferent pool monitors would let me drown; I couldn't go to the corner store with my friends because if one of them stole something, they would then accuse me and the police would put me in jail; if I played soccer, the team would leave me behind, on my own, alone on the field. In fact, that last situation did happen when I was about ten years old, and it reinforced their fears for my safety. According to their view, tragedy, injustice, and unfair treatment would follow me even when it came to innocently buying candy around the corner from our house. I couldn't see the danger they saw everywhere, and I was left time and again puzzled, angry, and sad.

Born in Paradox

My parents came from Haiti, where the fruits of imagination were everywhere to grasp while the political and religious leadership of the country discouraged, expelled, or even killed those expressing imagination or creativity outside the established norms of their times. Despite it all, in the way that people lived, survived, and spoke in Creole and French, the vivaciousness and humor of the people's imagination was fragrant, colorful, and fearlessly expressive, subverting the war on imagination taking place in their country. People there lived and sometimes thrived against all odds, and my parents brought that mentality of survival and dignity when they moved for good to Canada. But my parents were not culture hackers; if anything, they were very attached to their faith and religion.

Fitting In, Not Standing Out

I was born a few years after my parents emigrated to Canada, and I grew up in Montreal's East End with a distorted sense of what imagination was. I probably never heard the word *creativity* in the circles in which I grew up. If anything, I learned from my parents that imagination was suspicious and could bring trouble. It was an expression of arrogance, they thought, even blasphemy to make things up when our "Creator had already figured it all out" and a book had been written with prescriptions for all of us.

My parents wanted me to become a medical doctor like Marcus Welby M.D., the iconic TV doctor in the 1970s played by Robert Young. For a while, out of vanity and a need to please them, I aspired to become somebody that I fundamentally wasn't. They, like so many other parents before who had emigrated under immense stress and sacrifice, threw all their efforts in making sure that my younger brother Wendy, my sister Annie, and I fit in the new society they had adopted. Their core parental message was to never stand out, whatever we did, and to always fit in so we could stay out of trouble and go unnoticed.

In hindsight, they likely wanted us to be safe more than they wanted us to succeed because even that might have exposed us to the potential danger they saw everywhere. Security mattered more to them than entrepreneurial grit or creative courage, although they had risked it all by leaving their country to live in a sub-zero-degree climate. If I can observe this paradox in my parents' choices and priorities, it's hardly unique to them.

In fact, these are familiar tropes that many of us have been exposed to from an early age: *work hard; don't look too high; do your best to fit in; don't stand out; who do you think you are?* That message of conformism is not exclusive to immigrants. It's a message that sits at the core of our societies' need for control of the unknown, and under the wrong kind of leadership, it's a petri dish for the war on imagination to prosper. Blind conformism, unquestioned and never upgraded, is a creed that we find overtly or covertly expressed under the guise of celebrating individuals in every modern society, from the most conservative workplaces to many offices and headquarters considered to be paragons of creativity and innovation in the world.

My Personal War

Despite my parents' best intentions and their determination for me and my siblings to thrive, they unwittingly unleashed a similar war on imagination in our house. It was a war that I would observe and feel in my body and my bones many years later while eating Korean-style barbecue and cold noodles in the heart of North Korea.

The epicenter of that nameless war then, as I was heading toward preadolescence, found its most acute and painful expression in my confrontational and combustible relationship with my father. We didn't agree on much as I was growing up, and most of our disagreements would end in verbal or physical violence. He would exert his authority and rules-superabundant parenting in the way he had learned from his own father in Haiti by trying to stop any expression of dissidence from me with his hands and with a variety of objects.

I felt the effects of the war on imagination in a concrete way as a child and adolescent in and on my body. My father used violence as a way to beat the imagination out of me and keep my light from shining too brightly: *Fit in; conform; follow the rules; keep your voice down; work harder than anyone else; if you are not careful, you will be abandoned; with so many mistakes, it's almost too late for you now; wake up.* Every time he beat me, one or a combination of those messages was meant to enter my flesh, like a potent magical body lotion that left bold scarlet marks on my small frame as reminders for me to meditate on and pray through my tears.

My father didn't beat me out of love, nor out of cruelty, mercilessness, or pettiness but out of fear. He feared losing control of something he saw in me, a light that wasn't for him a source of orientation but something that would single me out, that would make me stand out in the world and bring trouble to my life. He saw in me the light that every kid has—the light of discovery and imagination, the source of our creative life force, the light that by its mere existence is already challenging the past and the status quo.

The war on imagination can emerge from the most positive intentions and legitimate goals. In my case, my father wanted to keep me safe and protect me from the discrimination that he suffered and from the harm of being denigrated. But his attempts at controlling my life made him the chief general of a war that nobody could win. The extent of that war expressed itself in concrete and disastrous ways. I was beaten with white electric extension cords, wet face cloths, a telephone. I was beaten with a kitchen table that perfectly fit the description of fake country antique. I was beaten with an oak bunk bed ladder that had two metal hooks to fix its body to the bed railings. I was beaten with a dark burgundy leather belt, a fine testament to the style meanderings of the 1970s. I find it curious and surprising looking back that a man like my father wore a belt that RuPaul himself might wear with aplomb and swagger today. I was beaten with a classic black leather belt, and a brown one and one with a big metal buckle celebrating the bold fashion of the 1980s, and with a badminton racket. I even had a kitchen slicing knife with a light green avocado handle pointed at my throat in a fit of anger.

I made furious, futile runs as I tried to escape the belts, hands, verbal invectives, and flying objects to dodge one more lash or hit.

My younger brother Wendy, agile in dark, resilient humor, joked some years later when we were adults that the only time my father got close to us or touched us during our childhood was to impose his will or frustrations by beating us.

There was no smart love at home, and the environment in which I grew up in was not conducive to any of us thriving; getting by was a better, more realistic option. Nobody could thrive through the impact of the war on imagination, waged with good intentions by my father and by forces much greater than him: not my dad, who was a high school teacher; not my mom, a pastry chef; not my brother or sister. Consequently, we became strangers to each other. We were bonded by our context and circumstances, but our links never deepened in intimacy, closeness, trust, or openness. Our family space had no sharable magic.

The Process of Creating Remarkable Communities

Perhaps because of my family experience steeped in pain, I became curious when I very young to learn more about what makes leaders and communities achieve remarkable, constructive things. Was there a way to lead, inspired by kindness, fairness, and real love rather than fear and despotic control? Without knowing anything about leadership, management, teamwork, success, or collaboration, my sensitivity to functioning at the highest level possible without inflicting psychological and physical abuse on anyone was emerging.

Church

Another source for my interest in the creation of positive communities came from the role that church played on my young mind during childhood. The experience of going to a place of worship, no matter the denomination, is connected, beyond faith, to building a sense of community, to belonging to a group. It's also about performances (singing, playing music, speaking, praying, sermonizing, teaching, debating). Both the sense of being part of a group of kindred spirits and the performances can play a role in the sensory happening and the rituals of each visit.

Learning about Good and Bad Performances

As a child, I could already see the impact of a good or a bad performance from a pastor on my parents and grandmother when we'd go to different churches. I'd often mentally compare notes. We'd go to the Pentecostal churches led by some members of the Haitian diaspora, nestled in the most improbable, inexpensive rental locations in Montreal, to the main church my family would eventually settle in, on Papineau Street near the subway of the same name and the gay village, established by locals, mixing Quebec-born citizens with immigrants from around the world; to the churches from myriads of denominations that we would visit from time to time for a wedding, a concert, or a funeral.

At four years old, as I imitated Elvis Presley in our living room with a carrot in hand as my microphone and an eight-track tape as my backup vocal, I intuitively yearned to understand not only the magic of perform-ance but also the process behind the magic.

Surreal, Scary Stories from My Parents' Homeland

Finally, another strong reason for that interest in process and results stemmed from my parents' lives as Haitian immigrants. For most of its history, Haiti has been led by so-called strongmen, dictators, and other authoritarian figures—colonial and then native. My parents had escaped the increasingly oppressive island in the 1970s. I was born a few years later in Montreal and have unfortunately visited Haiti only twice, at four and six years of age.

Despite my lack of familiarity with my parents' homeland, I was enthralled by the stories and news they would discuss with their friends and family, late at night, long after I was supposed to be in bed, about this notoriously ill yet beautiful, magical, obstinate country. The stories and news they shared were scary, heartbreaking, funny, and often surreal. There was the story of how my grandfather had stopped the rain to allow my young father to walk through a forest near Gonaives so he could get to an exam without getting wet. There was the story of the friends of the students' associations who would suddenly disappear, never to be seen again, and the fear of the Tonton Macoute, a special operations force, ruthless and brutal, that policed the country under their own arbitrary and cruel rules, even snatching kids to make them disappear (the force's name comes from a mythological Haitian Creole character who kidnaps children).

There were also other stories that we couldn't talk about because they involved too much magic, and that too was suspicious at home. In essence, though, they were stories not so different from those shared around the world on hardship and the will to rise beyond suffering. Around the kitchen table, my parents and their friends from time to time yearned for and dreamed and fantasized that Haiti would transform itself and finally get its affairs in order. They would tell those stories in disbelief, in irony, laughing and crying at the same time.

In my child's mind and heart, as I heard these stories not meant for me, I often dreamed that perhaps I could find a solution to these problems and sources of heartbreak for my parents. I would wonder if I could find a way to fix my parents' country. Maybe, as a ten-year-old, I could take a plane during the night, I could go there and talk to those people in power, convince them that a better way was possible. As a child emissary, I would speak truth and sense to power! *What if goodwill and love could change everything?* I wondered as I lay awake. My parents, particularly my dad, would be so proud of my heroic efforts. I wanted to do something impossible and beautiful for them.

I dreamed, as a child, of nothing less than saving an entire country, my parents' country, fantasizing that after such a feat, our family life would certainly be more peaceful and the conflict with my father less frequent. In radical contrast, and more in line with my age I had another vibrant dream, this one of dancing in one of Michael Jackson's videos. In fact, this happened when I started giving open-air break-dance classes in my neighborhood at Parc Liébert next to my elementary school in Montreal. It was also in that school that I performed, dressed as a highly approximate, improvised Michael Jackson look-alike for the kindergartners.

To Be Like MJ

Although 1984 marked the beginning of the video clip era in Canada, the access to videos was only occasional, as TV was in our home. Nonetheless, I had somehow found a way to study Michael Jackson's videos and moves. Even though I didn't look anything like the famous superstar, my teacher had organized a few shows for me to perform. Apparently, after my performance, the kids thought that I was the real Michael Jackson, despite my broken English and my royal blue baseball bomber jacket, dark pants, white socks, and running shoes.

I'd learn about the power of storytelling with the half-baked staging of my entrance in the kindergarten class. With my relatively small cassette tape player, offering to the audience the option of "Beat It" on one side and

"Billy Jean" on the other side of the BASF cassette, I would tell the class, half in invented English, half in French, with a fabricated high-pitched voice, that I could stay for only one performance since my helicopter was waiting for me outside to continue on to a world tour. The kids screamed with enthusiasm, and I magically made them travel with me to this imaginary world where for about four minutes, Michael Jackson had come to visit their class despite his extremely busy schedule. I remember the rush of adrenaline before and after showing my skills, and the eyes of the kids admiring my moonwalk, spins, and signature moves. I would leave the class shaking and proud. Through the power of imagination and play, we had transformed our lives for a few moments.

When my father learned about my dance performance at school, he profoundly disapproved. I was living parts of the similar story of a punishing, strict father in *Footloose* or *Billy Elliot* before these movies were released and long before I could see them myself. For my father and for our church, dance was suspicious; it meant moving with the unknown, the invisible. Dance was also insidiously sensual and therefore sexual, a sacrilege that could put you in touch with unseen forces and take control of your body. Dance was not serious but it was dangerous; it was the language of thugs and others who didn't respect the sanctity of order. Dance meant using your imagination to move molecules around you, and if my grades at school were not as good as they should be, it was probably because of the distractions of dance. Dance had nothing to do with my future success, and it needed to be stopped. My father did his best to get dance out of me, trying at times to physically remove it as if it were clothing too large for my body.

Masters of Illusion

A few years would go by and I kept wanting to dance, and it kept creating trouble for me. Never short on the only kind of stories that the war on imagination relishes, I was accused of "bringing Satan in a place of worship" when I tried to show friends at church how to do the break-dance windmill moves (in fact, I didn't really know how to do the move, and I should have been accused instead of bragging and lying). I had also secretly formed a break-dance crew near the end of elementary school, and we had all managed to save enough money by various means to buy a wonderful navy blue, white-striped Adidas crew windbreaker with "Masters of Illusion" printed on the back.

Every day, I hid the coat in my schoolbag, left home, turned the street corner, looked behind me, changed sidewalks, got closer to the baseball bleachers next to the park where I gave break-dance classes, and quickly changed coats, becoming one of the masters of illusion. At the end of the school day, I changed coats again before making my way home.

I remember the feeling of walking with my crew one day after school, intoxicated by the sensation of oneness and coolness that emanated from all of us. The girls, the other kids, the teachers: everyone smiled at our nascent swag. I felt free on those modest, working-class streets of eastern Montreal. I'd forget for a moment the many confrontations with my father. Now, I was one of the masters of illusion, and the war on imagination didn't exist. What if we were the next sensation to drop on the world? Montreal East, the new hub for talent after Brooklyn!

That's when my father suddenly emerged, like a dark force, from a street corner in his bright blue Ford Mercury Monarch, and angrily summoned me home. I was visibly scared and ashamed in front of my friends. At our house, I reluctantly gave up my beloved secret jacket, as my father requested, and he ripped it apart, like a violent surgery, separating in front of my eyes the words "Masters of" from "Illusion." It's as if my dad had ripped my heart out and scarred any future attempts at reconciliation between us.

The war on imagination was taking its toll on my spirit, and the resounding message sounded something like: "Don't dance, and don't bring that silly, dangerous magic home."

The Inner War

Over time, through escalating conflicts with my father, I was forced to make a choice that most kids continue to be asked to make as soon as possible, indirectly or directly, between imagination and factual, literal reality. In that sense, I could be either creative or pragmatic, artistic or organized, dreamer or focused, right brain or left brain. There were no acceptable or serious bridges between imagination and reality. The world was apparently sealed from any serious communication between these dimensions, and I was told that the one that prevailed, which had to do with hard, concrete facts and data, had more market value. *We can't choose to be both, so choose and be, wisely* was the meme. The war on imagination forced choosing sides.

In part, the logic behind this thinking was the idea that the skills of reasoning and pragmatism are something that you work to acquire. This demands an investment of efforts, even pain, to integrate, and therefore have nobility from not being easily accessible. Acquiring the ability of reasoning promises to forge character over time, whereas imagination and creativity are mostly connected to the artistic life, or to the archetype of gifted geniuses like Mozart, J. K. Rowling, and Nelson Mandela. The notion that the only way you could be gifted for creativity was naturally— that it was given to you, that you didn't really work for it—added suspicion to something already deemed fuzzy and difficult to measure.

The Falling Wall

On November 9, 1989, a vivid and irresistible rush of life force and hope filled my heart as I witnessed, with hundreds of millions of other people around the world, the beginning of the fall of the Berlin Wall. I was sixteen years old, and the metaphor of a mighty oppressive wall chipped at and breaking apart was uplifting, empowering, and a validation that I should seek more freedom within my own life. I felt that it was time to break the constraints on my own existence.

Looking back at my emotional reaction to the radical political changes around the fall of the wall in Berlin, I see how much it felt for me as the end of the war (on imagination) and the beginning of a new movement connecting different people and different ideas into something original and positive. I remember crying from the promise of reconciliation between people I didn't know but who had considered each other as enemies. I was elated, and I transported that enthusiasm at home, only to find the wall between my father and me taller than before, as if some of the snipers and checkpoints of the Berlin Wall had moved into our house after being evicted from Germany. The potential for incidents grew to the point that daily, the entire family suffered from bruises and discontent over the confrontations between my father and me. There was more violence for even much less of a reason and the newly open wound on my bedroom door—the trace of a fist leaving an irregular puncture that was my father's exclamation mark during a recent argument—was a reminder of how unstable peace and emotional safety had become in our home. What I was losing in imagination, I was gaining in distorted courage.

One night, I lost my creative courage, and the war almost won.

On April 10, 1990, at the age of sixteen, five months after the emotional euphoria I had experienced as I watched East and West Germany trying to move beyond their divisions, I tried to kill myself. I failed.

That day, after several weeks of falling downward, I became a casualty of the war on imagination after internalizing that conflict inside me. The only belief I had left was the dubious courage to quit. I no longer wanted to pursue what was beautiful. Questions, answers, and emotions didn't matter to me anymore.

But that day I failed at failing and faced a second chance at creating a more meaningful life. It would take years to untangle myself from the war on imagination, but slowly and progressively, I emerged with a new outlook on life and work. I know that what we choose to do can be important and meaningful for ourselves and others, despite the fear of rejection that never completely goes away.

At home and abroad, the challenge on imagination remains. The war on imagination in my home made the magic of discovering life's mysteries and secrets, growth, even love more difficult to experience, integrate, and benefit from. Although innovation, discoveries, and breakthroughs can happen in the most abject conditions, they are much harder to taste, celebrate, and sustain in a toxic environment where the war festers. In North Korea, for instance, I felt intuitively in many fellow humans there the same hidden despair stemming from pretending to be "all right" and to be invincible, and the covert but real yearning for light, love, and belonging that most human beings thrive on.

The war on imagination tries to build a wall to seal imagination away from reality, but unless you build a wall that doesn't have a door, effectively locking yourself in from the outside world, there's always an opening and therefore a chance for the wall to be breached or, metaphorically, for hope, light, and unity to emerge again.

I left North Korea with a sense that although you can build the most elaborate, monumental walls, like a virtual prison, there are always cracks to let some of the light in and for people to not be locked in forever. The jailer never sleeps in the cell.

Harmful work conditions stemming from what I call the war on imagination will make it more difficult to thrive and create products and services of meaningful impact, no matter where you live or work. Still more pernicious, the war on imagination creates the most devastation when we integrate its codes inside ourselves. It affects our capacity to grow constructively and to work with more influence and meaning. At the other end of the spectrum, creativity as a tool and a trigger of innovations can produce important, sustainable impact.

 ## II. Insights

The War at Work

We don't all live in North Korea, and not everyone had to struggle with abuse and violence at home; nonetheless, the war on imagination affects many among us and eventually creeps into our work. Sir Ken Robinson, the internationally known British arts education professor, famously said, "All children start their school careers with sparkling imaginations, fertile minds, and a willingness to take risks with what they think. . . . Most students never get to explore the full range of their abilities and interests. . . . Education is the system that's supposed to develop our natural abilities and enable us to make our way in the world. Instead, it is stifling the individual talents and abilities of too many students and killing their motivation to learn."[2]

In the context of nurturing our creative courage, we could add to Sir Ken Robinson's invitation to reignite in our schools the "motivation to learn," the desire to discover, to move beyond the unknown. This process of disconnection from our potential for imagination, and therefore with our creativity in school while growing up, can find an exceptionally fertile ground at work. The war on imagination is pervasive; it knows no discrimination based on gender, socioeconomic background, geography, or personal history. Through the erosion from the war on imagination, I had lost my drive to learn, create, and solve problems. The connection to my creative courage was missing because I didn't understand then that it wasn't a destination to reach, but a mind-set to cultivate and revisit as often as possible. It was the foundation for a set of practices that could form an antidote against the war on imagination, against losing my creative courage and for making it stronger.

A Clash at the Heart of Our Brand

The conditions for the war on imagination to damage our experience at work takes a familiar shape that can be as damaging as when we suffer from it in our personal lives. Its symptoms can affect both the organization and the individuals who work in it.

Typically the context necessary for the war to grow starts with a clash between a company's legacy on one hand and its need to continue to grow on the other hand. The more a company understands about its heritage and the reason for its past or current relevance, the more it can grow; it can then let go of that past or at least not hold on to it so hard. The more its past serves as a cane to justify the relevance of its existence rather than a strong reference to its foundation, the more it puts growth in the future at risk. This clash between its past, present, and future offers opportunities to increase its influence on the world; it can also introduce the risk of becoming overly defensive about its assets and eventually lose ground and importance. If you add to this background a more autocratic style of leadership and a closed, noninclusive, diversity-averse process for decision making, arrogance can quickly develop and, with it, the belief that all answers come only from inside of the company. It leads constituents, employees, team members, and eventually clients and customers to progressively lose faith in the ability of the company to affect the world positively. In fact, all of these constituents also start to lose the belief in their own capacity to leverage imagination and creativity to solve problems and meet challenges in their environment. They lose something akin to what David Kelley and Tom Kelley call "creative confidence."[3]

Manifestations of the War on Imagination at Work

If confidence is something that you build over time, courage stems from a decision that you take right now. It can last as little as ten seconds yet be powerful enough to trigger a path toward eventual confidence. Courage, in other words, precedes confidence. Confidence is a by-product, the outcome, stemming from the decision to practice courage. Without that creative courage, fear sets in.

At the level of the organization, the business becomes hostile to creativity and imagination not because it is heartless but because it is afraid. Creativity can start to sound like an expensive waste of time and resources. At the level of the individual in the organization, the toxic effects of the war on imagination can take many forms, even if they appear benign and inconsequential. For example, it happens when we are in a meeting and keep our mouth shut because we think that our idea is stupid or not worth sharing, or that we are not qualified or high enough in the hierarchy to share our views. At times, our organization will actively or covertly send us the same message that our views, opinions, and aspirations don't matter, for whatever reason.

I meet casualties of the war on imagination almost every day whenever I hear someone tell me that he or she is "not creative" before expressing an idea, or as an explanation for not sharing her views on a given situation, challenge, or problem. When we are not connected to our creative potential, no matter what work we do, we fall for one of the most damaging effects of the war: we disengage, and that disengagement becomes the status quo, the default position.

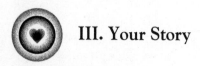 **III. Your Story**

Disconnection with Imagination at Work

My experience has led me to see, at times, in myself and in colleagues or partners a palpable disconnection from our creativity and sense of imagination. This disconnection is prevalent across different work cultures, industries, and disciplines. I've tracked six main symptoms or false beliefs that help identify the presence of elements of the war on imagination at work. Whenever these are present, the risks for the war to expand grow.

False Belief 1. I'm Not Creative

This is the most common statement I hear: only certain people are creative. Often we feel this way because the process behind leveraging creativity and imagination is obscure and mysterious and we connect them exclusively to professional artistic practices.

"I'm not creative" can take on different meanings depending on the situation. Here are a few examples:

- I'm too serious, rigorous, scientific, organized [etc.] to be creative.
- I can't draw.
- I'm color-blind.
- I hate fashion.
- I only paint as a hobby.
- I can't dance.
- I'm on the business side of the company.
- I'm not a creative genius like you are.
- I don't have ideas.
- I take care of operations.
- I don't know anything about this situation.
- I can't do trapeze.
- I can't sing.
- I can't dream.
- I can't be organized, structured, and creative at the same time [and vice versa].

False Belief 2. Only Artists Are Creative

This is the greatest confusion I've noticed and something that continues to be encouraged by our culture and education system. Being creative for many is the equivalent of being an artist. Images of the liberal arts or the performing arts emerge to delight or conjure fear in the minds of those blurring the line between the two. The confusion confining creativity to art is sad both for artists who want to meet an audience that's as creative as possible and for all the nonartists who should remember that every child is inherently creative.

The war on imagination creates a mask that makes people disconnect from their creativity at work, which discourages the basic needs for accountability, engagement, and a sense of initiative that businesses yearn to find in their employees. It's a huge disservice to our culture and a false belief that's hard to dispel that only artists are creative. At its most fundamental expression, life itself is an incarnation of creativity, and all of us can become a vector, a medium of that creative energy, harnessing it for work and for our life.

False Belief 3. Creativity Is Scarce

Creativity and the fruits of imagination are scarce and therefore need to be carefully shared or kept secret; otherwise the well of ideas will soon tarnish. I've witnessed collaborators so insecure about their ideas, creativity, and artistry that they struggled to share the fruits of their talents with their teammates and the projects they were working on. They approached creativity, imagination, and ideas from a standpoint of extreme limitation rather than abundance and possibility.

I certainly was a culprit of waiting for the right moment to develop an idea, keeping it sealed in my heart or in a notebook, only to discover later that someone else also had had that idea and had taken the time to develop it further. The beautiful and unsettling truth is that ideas are plentiful, and they will visit anyone ready not only to host them but also to develop them and make them grow.

False Belief 4. I'm the Special One, the Only One Who Can Be Creative

When you are more in touch with your creativity and since not everyone enjoys the same level of intimacy with that aspect of themselves, you run a risk of becoming exclusive in the way you develop your gift. The war on imagination is never far away when we think that creativity and imagination come through us exclusively. By definition, creativity and imagination have everything to do with generosity above egoism. Creating from a place where you are the only person perceived as having something special comes with advantages (adulation, admiration, deference, fascination), although it doesn't maximize the potential of the project as a source of growth for the collective. If everyone is creative, you might ask, then what makes *me* special? My answer is that being creative is not so much about being special but about having a special, original, courageous relationship with what's inside and around us. In that sense, it's a lie to think that it's about our own specialness more than it is about what's special through our eyes and heart, a progressively more intimate connection with the unknown.

False Belief 5. Creativity Is a Waste of Time—It Offers No Return on Investment, No Value

I've witnessed how dangerous it can be to expect the fruits of imagination to flourish without proper watering and wise patience. This always makes leveraging imagination and creativity for innovation hard in a business context. Although you need to capture as much of it as possible through typical management tools, its essence will remain unfathomable to spreadsheet and return on investment data analysis. It resists straight-jackets yet in the proper context, it is a great power to counter the effects of the war on imagination. The path that creativity proposes rarely takes the shape of a straight, unobstructed line.

False Belief 6. In Results Only We Trust: Creativity in Result but Not in Process

No matter what the human cost is, only results matter. The entertainment industry is notorious for being primarily concerned with the outcome rather than the process that leads to it. If you have any doubt about that, consider the many stars who end up destroyed by the industry that brought them fame and fortune. It's true not only for stars; this applies as well to people working backstage, supporting those who are in the spotlight. In other words, until recently, it didn't matter so much how a show was created, how a star was prepared for a tour, or what it took for the crew to make it to the premiere. *The show had to go on*, and that usually meant by any means necessary. If some people weren't making it to the end or made it there but were somewhat damaged, it didn't matter much as long as the result was spectacular.

This *show must go on* mind-set is not restricted to the entertainment world; in most organizations, our attitude toward the end justifying the means applies as well. In sports, it's not uncommon to hear that if the team wins and everyone does their jobs, it doesn't matter if people get abused, an unfortunate mentality that is omnipresent in our culture despite our aspirations to change it.

I'm uniquely driven about the result of what I create, but I wanted to understand more and improve how we reach our outcomes, however great or small. Progressively over the last twenty years, I have made it my passion to work hard at understanding what makes memorable work stick in the hearts and minds of both audiences and the people creating it. I believe that my desire for improving the quality of our process when creating great work is relevant not only for people evolving in the traditionally assigned creative sectors, but for anyone working with a group, small or big, or in the business world working with teams, collaborators, or partners. How can you improve the process of creating your work, and how can improving that process create value, inside and out, for the people on your team and those you are working to serve (e.g., customers, clients)? How can you forge ahead with amazing work without having people lose part of who they are or more during the work cycle? How can you transform your work beyond your wildest dream?

Scanning Your Team, Project, Business, and Organization

During the sixteen years that I've spent working at Cirque du Soleil, I've experienced the glorious energy of an organization dedicated to surpassing its unique heritage of imagination and outstanding creativity every day. I've also lived through moments when the war on imagination took too much space, threatening the resilience and the relevance of such an extraordinary company.

No one and no organization is beyond the risk of suffering from such a war; no organization is ever perfect. I believe that creative courage as a mind-set and a conscious decision to constantly go back to a spirit of humility, curiosity, and determination toward the unknown is an attitude that opens doors to practices and activities that can strengthen our work and how people grow within it. Over the years, I have assembled these practices and activities into a framework inspired by my view of creative courage. Most of us say that we value innovation, imagination, creativity, and collaboration at work, but how do we know if our work culture promotes or discourages imagination, beyond the talking point, the PR operations, and the branding savvy? How do we know if the war on imagination happens at work, and what can we do to fix it, improving the situation and reaching beyond our wildest dreams? Either the war on imagination is kept at bay, and we can use the framework to fortify our organization against it, or we can realize that the war is front and center and we can also use the framework to fight back with creative courage.

Here are a few questions to use to quickly and intuitively scan your work, your team, your organization and assess the presence—or not—of the war on imagination:

- How do you qualify the general leadership of your organization or business (it can obviously be a mix of the strongest attributes)?
  - Responsive (feedback and discussion leads to improvement)
  - Accessible (open-door policy)
  - Inclusive (actively consulting at multiple levels of the organization)
  - Autocratic (hard to voice your disagreement or to correct course if you see things going wrong)
  - Secretive (you don't know what's going on and care less and less, disengaging; note that organizations that are simply bad at communicating with their teams end up giving the same impression of secrecy even if the intention is different)
- If you are one of the executive leaders of the organization, are you typically accessible or difficult to reach for your team, partners, clients, and others, no matter what the reasons are?
- How upfront and proactive is the organization in dealing with the good news (celebration) and bad news with its personnel?
- Do you consider your organization excellent, good, or weak at dealing constructively with facts and perceptions if those facts and perceptions are negative, neutral to its image, and positive to its image? Are there any notable differences between the categories of facts and perceptions?
- Do you find that your time for reflection versus your time for action is optimal, excellent, fair, or inadequate?
- How much tension exists in your organization between past successes and history and the need for growth and relevance in the present and future? Is there a lot of nostalgia about how things were or instead great clarity on the company's current purpose?
- Who's your sage, your Yoda (the old and famous *Star Wars* Jedi)? Do you have a sage, a wise man or wise woman, a group of mentors within your organization you can access easily? Is this a formal or informal structure within your organization? In either case, how easy is it to access such resources when they are needed?

- On a scale of 1 to 10, 10 being the highest, how much care do you think people use to work with each other in your business? Do you think that care and high performance are somewhat in contradiction, the two faces of the same coin, or something in between?
- Do you recognize any of the false beliefs listed previously in you or within your organization? List them. Do you know of other false beliefs that it might be worth listing here as well?

The war on imagination at work will affect the ability of your leadership to be more inclusive and visionary by struggling to include diverse points of view and agile integration of feedback from the outside world on its activities. In addition, the war on imagination will take a bigger toll on teams, groups, and individuals when there's an disproportionate amount of time devoted to thinking in relation to action, either because we think too much without making things happen or inversely because we are constantly in action mode with little or no space for deep reflection and deep work. Finally, and most fundamentally, the war on imagination at work will intensify when the harmony and natural tension between the past success and heritage of an organization and its most pressing questions in the present (Where do we go from here? How do we grow now?) start to lose their harmony, becoming instead dissonant and conflictual. Typically, in such a scenario, the company's purpose becomes blurry, and the exclusive focus on the bottom line replaces it. The more your answers to the questions listed tend to outline a disharmony of time and consciousness, of past and present, the more likely it is that the invisible war on imagination has taken hold. If that is the case, do not despair; transformation is always possible when there's a will to put a shining, benevolent spotlight on the issues we face.

If your answers to this quick scan demonstrates that your organization tends toward harmony, congratulations. The path ahead could still inspire you to fortify your projects, team, and business with the spirit of creative courage.

A Path of Seven Stages

At its core, practicing creative courage unbars the path to a sequence of evolving and infinitely open cycles composed of seven integrated stages that represent as many dimensions of creative courage and that comprise an array of practices, questions, tools and tips that you can augment, improve and adapt to your unique situation. To rise beyond the war on imagination or to prevent its outbreak, we start by *caring first* (Chapter 2) and *securing safety* within the team (Chapter 3). Caring and safety allow you to move forward effectively and with confidence in *fostering trust* (Chapter 4) because of your groundwork. You can then start to experiment with *playing with danger and limitations* (Chapter 5) to unlock the ability of your team to *dream* (Chapter 6) boldly, more generously, dreams that can lead to discover real breakthroughs (Chapter 7), which allows you, your employees, your audience, your clients, and your business to *grow* (Chapter 8).

With time, this can become a virtuous circle, allowing the practices that you already master to be integrated into that framework. I finish with an example, *start to dance* (chapter 9), that puts all these stages together, in a personal way, to transform the outcome of the war on imagination.

The practices, outlook, tools, and tips under the umbrella of creative courage offer a powerful framework that you can adapt to your reality as you help yourself and your organization transform while staying true to your most important principles. Leading with creative courage offers support on the path to inside-out importance for you and your brand, however big or small.

You can implement actions at any of the seven stages, although their sequence means that the strength of one stage is related to the strength of what precedes it. For example, if you identified that work needs to be done in securing safety within your team, your success can improve if you have worked diligently on assessing where you are with the caring first practices, and so on.

Summary

Creative courage is the mind-set triggered by the decision to embrace the unknown without having all of the answers. Because this condition is inherent to life itself, we have in all of us the potential to activate our creative courage. It's also an umbrella term for a set of practices and activities aimed at supporting an environment fertile for holistic creativity and innovation.

Creative courage opens routes to move through the fear of failure toward the joy of bringing something essential to our life and that of others. To our conventional concerns about our bottom line, we add a high line that considers relevance, meaning, and resonance for the people that we create for and ultimately benefit from our work. Relevance becomes the ultimate currency. Through the practice of leading with creative courage, we realize how precious valuing the bottom line and the high line of our organization is. Profit and relevance unite.

One of the greatest challenges of our time lies in the tension that emerges from the dialogue between the past and the present. This pressure is one of the most important sources of creativity and innovation. Although the potential for innovation rises when that tension is exacerbated, the risk of confusion, isolation, and conflict rises as well. Coupled with an autocratic or a myopic leadership (focused on the necessary bottom line but not on the vital high line, the visionary work), the risk of a war on imagination, a war on the potential for creativity, innovation, and breakthrough at work, is high. But this is not inevitable; there are ways to fight back, reclaim our sacred and innate sense of imagination, and courageously transform or reinvigorate our work into a well of meaning and a source of real value, for us and for those that we work for and with.

In a few words, the war on imagination has these characteristics:

- Dysfunctional leadership
- Clash of the past and the present at work, making your brand unclear to manage and grow
- Speed anomaly: little or no time to think, reflect, and step back
- Deliberate unawareness: organizational denial or refusal to address facts and perceptions about itself

This book offers a sequential, incremental, evolving path and framework to transform work:

Stage 1. Care first

Stage 2. Secure safety

Stage 3. Foster trust

Stage 4. Play with danger and limitations

Stage 5. Dream

Stage 6. Discover breakthroughs

Stage 7. Grow

Note that this is not *the* only path but *a* path that I propose based on my experience, discussions with hundreds of leaders from a variety of industries, observations and interpretations, and inspiration from other authors and thinkers. I have conceived this path of stages with open source as a quality in mind. It has the potential to be used in any organization, large or small, as a simple work grid for evaluating, assessing where you are, and identifying the strengths and weaknesses of your approaches to innovation and leadership, which I believe are profoundly linked.

The order of the practices suggests the beginning and the end of a loop that keeps growing, within you and with your business, and that you can review or update whenever you need to. In other words, there will never be a time during the life of your organization when you will be able to say that you have cared enough, dreamed enough, or grown enough. It's also an incremental path that proposes a relationship between what precedes and what follows. For example, it's harder to play with danger and limitations when trust is too deficient. Trust goes beyond demonstrated safety and denotes a living, dynamic relationship of give and take. Trust goes beyond the transactional and moves to the emotional. In the same spirit, growth follows discovering breakthroughs because typically it's hard to grow without a breakthrough. It doesn't mean that things are perfect, only that there's enough care and safety in the bank to live and work through trust.

Of course, you can enter at any stage and develop from there and take ideas, do exercises, and get inspired by the practices that I propose. But it's important to keep in mind that one stage will only be as strong as the one that precedes it. Finally, the stronger and more in shape your previous stages are, the better you can reinforce the stage you want to reach.

CHAPTER 2

Care First

Respect Is Not the First Step When Disengagement Is the Status Quo

Attention is the rarest and purest form of generosity.

Simone Weil[1]

I. Raising the Curtain

The most prevalent example of the war on imagination at work finds its expression in the disengagement that executives and other employees can feel and act on. Left unchecked, disengagement becomes the status quo and leads to a vicious circle. When we shut down, we create a lack of transparency and a scarcity of open communication, work in silos festers, and cynicism affects everyone in a downward spiral. The word *disengagement* has profound implications, not only for weakening the potential that exists in our work but also the greater context of our social and economic fabric. From my standpoint, to be disengaged means to be disconnected and skeptical of our ability to create positive change in our lives or to have a positive contribution to our environment. In other words, to be disengaged is to let go of our creative courage. We accept internally and collectively the belief that we can't change our lives, the sources of our pain, and the challenges or problems ahead of us. We disengage from our potential to create and innovate.

Let's use our imagination and pretend for a moment that we are in Paris. It's February 13, 2017, on the eve of Valentine's Day in the Western world and some Asian countries as well. It's also nighttime, and riots are happening in two neighborhoods on the city's edges. Here, a corner store has been vandalized, and boxes, fruits, and vegetables are strewn over the floor. A car nearby is on fire and in the background is a police squad in full anti rampage regalia, alert. That night, fewer than a hundred young people in that Paris suburb, feeling left behind, angry, even bored, decided to break things and act out their sense of exclusion, unfairness and alienation.

The conundrum in that situation is that these devastating acts of destruction and violence are a desperate but myopic attempt to change the state of things. They exhibit a reckless, destructive engagement and, at the same time, are the ultimate expression of a status quo where disengagement is the new normal. Although it doesn't usually take similar forms in the workplace, that disengaged status quo exists at work and can have damaging impact there too. You don't need a riot in the corridors of your workplace to feel the war on imagination flex its muscle through workforce disengagement.

The following morning, responding to the crisis at the heart of his capital, French President François Hollande urged respect from citizens and police alike as a way to calm things down. During a press conference near one of the riot sites, he said:

> *There is no life as a community if there is no respect. These young people deserve respect when they are stopped for police identity checks, when they themselves are confronted with violent situations. Respect.*
>
> *We must all be respectful of institutions—the police, the justice system. . . .*
>
> *We also need to show respect for public and private property. And if there are demonstrations—and the right to demonstrate freely exists in France— it is not permission to wreak havoc.*[2]

Where Respect Starts

The real dilemma is that respect, like love, is harder to give when you've never received it. It's hard to give the respect that you feel you've never received, perhaps because you genuinely don't even know what it is. Moreover, if you've never received much care, it's tough to care and even tougher to give care back. But where does respect start if everyone is expecting it from someone else? Rightfully, the police expect it from the young people in Paris. With full legitimacy, the young people await that same respect from the police; and the citizens from their government, the employees from their employers, and so on. So where does the virtuous circle start if everyone expects the other person and the other group to move first?

Caring First

I argue that it starts with having the creative courage of caring first. Since the law of reciprocity must start somewhere, it can start with you, with us as leaders, through the decision of practicing creative courage to care first. Respect is one of the outcomes of something greater, or at least something that precedes it: care. My proposition is that the creative courage to care first can eventually lead to respect as a desired by-product, though not as the initial prize. Moving with creative courage in this case means moving beyond the fear and pain of being a victim, of falling short in the exchange to offer care first. In many ways, it's daring and counterintuitive, and it goes against the concept of tit-for-tat.

Disengagement at Work

In situations of disengagement at work, we tend to expect respect first from team members, collaborators, and other employees—respect to the brand, to investors, to the leaders, to commitments, objectives, to key performance indicators, to colleagues, to deadlines, to the investments that the company made in the project, and more. Although respect matters greatly, things start with care, not respect. Like love, respect is not something that truly gets enforced through force; only fear can be imposed that way. No one knows for sure what would happen if the squalid, psychologically toxic environments of the suburbs where people just survive in France and elsewhere were thoroughly bombed with beauty, opportunity, and other forms of care. I like to think that the war on imagination that's taking place every day would have less chance of perpetrating its ravages if that were the case.

Space Matters

If we accept as true that caring first precedes respect to increase the chance that a forgotten suburb in France can thrive, it's also true in the context of creating and nurturing innovative and innovating workplaces able to optimize their creativity and imagination. From that standpoint, space matters. Teams need space to work, dream, meet, play, do nothing, and do everything.

You probably know and apply many principles of designing a great space for creative work, so I will try to offer something beyond the usual ideas of a table tennis table and beanbag chairs. (We will look at this in more detail in Chapters 5 and 6 on how to become more intentional about space to support the creative process and the innovation output.) There is a profound link between the impact of great spaces or squalid ones in the streets of a Parisian suburb and the effect of your space on building your capacity to create more.

Dark Outcomes

Workplace disengagement echoes differently from what we witness on TV and in the streets. Most often, the disenchantment and anger portrayed in the street offer something visually sensational that sells and scares. Its impacts are nonetheless far from innocuous. From common burnout to important drops in productivity and increased absenteeism, subtle yet devastating effects of the war on imagination like cynicism, negativism, and dis-engagement can go as far and as dark as suicides in the workplace from employees desperate to end the pain and the liabilities of a supremely toxic environment.[3] Disengagement is real, and its outcome can be dire.

Disengagement Close to Home

On January 16, 2013, the Canadian Broadcast Company and most of the media outlets across Canada announced just past noon that Cirque du Soleil was letting go four hundred employees across its organization. Just about a month earlier, the top executives of the company had offered me the job of leading the creation of Cirque's second show on the theme of Michael Jackson.

If the first show, *Immortal: The World Tour*, led by another talented team based in Montreal, had faced outsized expectations way before its opening on October 2011, the challenge for this new project was of a different order. First, there's always a different type of pressure when a show is set to open permanently in Las Vegas, Cirque du Soleil's second home. Typically, the investment in time and resources and the return on investment for these shows brings the bar higher than on any other projects. In addition, Michael Jackson had visited several Cirque du Soleil shows in Las Vegas, and the entire creative team as well as the Michael Jackson Estate wanted to leave a legacy show close to Michael's last home, in Los Angeles. If the stakes were not high enough, this sad news of layoffs, the most important in Cirque's history, was affecting morale among all the employees.

The Context

Despite Cirque's outstanding global success, wide cultural resonance, and economic growth since the mid-1990s and later in 2000 with the arrival of CEO and president Daniel Lamarre, the landscape of the company had changed. The world had seen an economic crisis, the transformation of audiences, and the impact of close to twenty years of almost uninterrupted growth on Cirque's organizational structure and management style. More-over, Cirque du Soleil was now in competition with every other enter-tainment form rather than benefiting from being in a category of its own.[4]

Part of its future growth would involve having to go through an eventual sale of its assets to new investors, which in fact happened in spring 2015.

Meanwhile, the war on imagination was showing its scary head. From a leadership forced to focus on the bottom line but challenged to integrate visionary work at the same time to a sense that despite the greatness of the company's past and its strong present, the future was for the first time uncertain, blurry, and scary for some. Suddenly nostalgia took hold for some, while others became cynical, even bitter. To no one's fault, the workforce was full of doubt and skeptical of the company's initiatives.

It's with this context as our background that I accepted my nomination as creative director of the show in creation, *Mandalay 2013*, named for the MGM hotel in Las Vegas that was going to host the show. This project would later become the hit show *Michael Jackson ONE*. For several reasons, we broke a few agreed-on paradigms in the creation of this show. For example, typically thirty-six months were needed to create a show in Las Vegas, whereas now we had only eighteen months to the opening.

It was also then a principle not to repeat ourselves artistically, so once a show was created, we weren't duplicating that show as Broadway does, for example. Creating a second show on the same topic, Michael Jackson, even if it wasn't a duplication of *Immortal: The World Tour*, felt like a downward spiral or an abdication for some colleagues who were more nostalgic or believed that Cirque du Soleil should only create original work. The belief some held was that real artists and creators imagined only from scratch. Moreover, working with a brand as globally recognized as Michael Jackson felt for some that we were selling out as a company and losing our capacity to be creative.

I was indirectly and directly criticized for that, although these were not my decisions. I was also the youngest creative director at the time, and the one with zero experience on a show of that scale, so many wondered if I was the sacrificial lamb.

It is in such a context that the loss of four hundred employees, a first in the history of the company, was announced and resonated heavily throughout the group in Montreal, Las Vegas, and the rest of the world. Like any other company in that situation, we had to find ways to do things faster, with fewer resources and additional limitations challenging the status quo and the way things were usually done. The conditions were ripe for the war on imagination to take hold of the whole or for the creative courage in my heart to lead the way.

A New Situation without an Instruction Manual

We were also opening the eighth show on the Las Vegas Strip, and in the mind of many, one question reflected the subtext of an article later that year announcing our arrival: "Is Eight Too Much?" After the extraordinary success of the company, its founder's journey from humble beginnings to riches and a sense that with this new project in Las Vegas, the important loss of jobs, and the repeat with the Michael Jackson Estate, Cirque was perhaps losing its way. Those envious of its success wanted it to fail, and many who loved Cirque didn't want it to change. It was a new situation for us, something I had never experienced before, and my boss, the upcoming creative guide of the company, Jean-François Bouchard, made it clear that I had only one option despite it all: I had to find a way to succeed against all odds.

Caring First: The Team

The most powerful tool any leader can offer to practice caring first is to listen. Over the course of the project, but with added intent when I joined a team with some already in place (like my stellar production manager, Michel Rioux) mixed with new members like the superstar director Jamie King, I listened with deliberateness, took notes, and asked questions to understand them better. I benefited from being willing to listen to an extraordinary team to understand more about who they were, and not just what my perception of them was. At the heart of this deceptively simple yet challenging practice lies a crucial belief that is close to my heart. When I met the team members, I tried to listen not only to their words and ideas but also their superpowers and genius.

Superpowers in You

I believe that we universally share one superpower that doesn't need to be discovered but needs to be developed, like when we learn to swim, bike, or walk. We all have the superpower to become exceptional listeners to find common ground with others. We can use that super-power when we need to listen to what's happening inside (e.g., meditation, running, or writing as forms of inner listening) and can also direct it to others. Listening is a practice that grows over time and is a fundamental skill in discovering and supporting the growth of other people's superpowers and our own. I believe that each of us also has a set of superpowers that we can discover and develop. Those additional superpowers can be constructive or destructive depending on what we decide to do with them.

Instead of referring to "a skill inaccessible to humans therefore super-human," a *superpower* is an ability that adds an unexpected value to work while feeding one's aspirations directly or indirectly. It is available to anyone who dares to look, and it is distinctive to all of us. In addition to the ability to develop powerful listening, it is one of the cornerstones of the practice of caring first. Behind the apparent magical thinking of consider-ing our own superpowers lies a strong evidence base from the creative and artistic world as the power of affirmation. Anyone who's created anything knows that whatever artwork is created in the world has already been conceived in some way. We think about it, we dream about it, we conceive it by sketching it, maybe prototyping it before its eventual creation. Said differently, the artwork grows and exists in our mind before it finds its manifestation in the world, be it physical or virtual. That concept of creating something twice is not new but sometimes forgotten when we consider how affirmations work. In giving superpower properties to some of your most notable strengths, talents, and forces, you confer through affirmation something supernatural and sacred to what you can bring to your work. You symbolically take your skills a little bit more seriously without being too serious about it.

Aspirations in Superpowers

To build or support a truly creative and innovative force at work requires understanding your own inner aspirations and those of your colleagues, employees, and other team members. The key to discovering the superpowers hiding in plain sight in your team is to have a good grasp of their aspirations and yearnings, deep and profound, superficial and trivial. What are your deepest aspirations right now? What do you yearn for the most? It doesn't have to be related in any way to your work, but if you are willing to share what those deep aspirations and surface yearnings are, you will have a path to discover the most appropriate words to describe your own superpowers and those of the people that you care about and that surround you. This is where I started with my team during the creation of *MJ ONE*. I was constantly updating my mental and actual map of the team's superpowers.

I imagine at times that managing and leading a team for innovation and creativity is similar to juggling with three big rings. One represents your superpowers stemming from your aspirations, the second represents the superpowers and aspirations of your team, and the third represents the superpowers and aspirations of your company. The goal of the juggling act is to create a Venn diagram in midair, discovering the common ground that they create together. Leading becomes the constant realignment in midair, both beautiful and approximate, changing and evolving with time.

If we take seriously the aspirations and the superpowers of others, it is possible to do miraculous work. Because I spent time with the production manager to create the most conducive space possible for the individual talents on the team to shine for the project, we managed to quickly create a show that stayed memorable in the hearts of many. We confounded even the most skeptical.

But What about Them?

When I'm called to speak at conferences, I'm often asked by bewildered managers how I manage diversity (at Cirque du Soleil more than fifty nationalities are represented regularly) and what to do with millennials. Far from pretending to have all the answers or to suggest that circus artists or young artists from different disciplines are representative of the cohort of millennials, I nevertheless recognize something in them that's often associated with millennials: they want to thrive. In large part, I disagree with that characterization. Everybody wants to thrive; it just means something different for different groups and individuals based on their aspirations, deep and superficial, conscious and not.

Millennials, like any other group, can't be simply categorized as a group and labeled with limiting and misleading clichés. If anything, I share that from my observation of millennials, but I suspect that it might be true for anyone in touch with their creative courage: they don't want to be managed; they want to be inspired. I think that this is in line with the idea of discovering and then nurturing aspirations and superpowers with the radical proposition that it doesn't matter if they are related to the business or not.

You Don't Have to Be a Superhero to Have Superpowers

What's so compelling about superheroes in popular culture is that they usually have very clear strengths, superpowers, and aspirations. Wonder Woman wants to bring peace to the world and has the power to stop bullets with her bracelets and has the knowledge of some of the most ancient and secret combat techniques. Batman leverages his scientific knowledge and athletic abilities to foster his superhuman skills to save Gotham.

Of course, I'm not suggesting that we have superhero abilities, just that we have abilities, strengths, aspirations, and yearnings that can make a tremendous difference in creating remarkable work when they are taken seriously and when work becomes a playground for these superpowers to flourish. When we don't take that potential seriously, we discover situations similar to how Silicon Valley developed an important sexism problem after initially benefiting from the efforts of many female mathematicians and scientists who did the coding behind the more celebrated hardware and engineering work reserved to males. Reversing this trend will take years and cost many of the companies their legitimacy.

Added Support for the Practice of Caring First

One of my superpowers is my ability to lead with kindness while still being able to be real and candid, a practice I believe that most people can learn and that I call *real-kind*. When you own your superpowers, you can become intentional with them, and labeling them helps give you quick access to them when needed. To discover the superpower of real-kind, I had to use various tools and eventually developed an approach inspired by some of the instruments readily available in the marketplace, with my adaptations. (I share more later in this chapter about ideas to discover superpowers.)

As we accept that our workplace can become a place for team superpowers to flourish, the return on investment for the company can be surprising. Furthermore, the nurturing of your own superpowers and those of your team members can lead to two additional elements that support the practice of caring first, discussed next.

A Collective Superpower

When we work collaboratively or want to improve our ability to do so, discovering and celebrating the superpowers of individual team members is important. However, understanding the nature of the collective superpowers of your group is what makes the difference between a remarkable performance and one that's memorable for the ages. It requires leaders to characterize, based on their intuitive and factual understanding of individuals' superpowers, what could be the collective quality of the group and how best to empower it.

Most of us are familiar with sports teams that have assembled some of the best players in their sport thanks to the depth of their wallet and determination to win, only to bite the dust in the championship. I also think of the famous example of the Broadway musical *Spiderman: Turn of the Dark*, composed exclusively of superstars from the entertainment world like Bono and The Edge, Julie Taymor, and the superbrand Marvel, each with superpowers of their own but never able to truly rise as a collective and express their demonstrated genius. From my standpoint, the role of any leader is in part to make sense of that collective superpower, too often left dormant inside many organizations and projects.

Genius

People sometimes laugh when I say that they are geniuses. To this day, pronouncing that word conjures images of world figures like Picasso, Einstein, Grace Hopper, Marie Curie, and Nelson Mandela. Not only are we not usually in touch with our individual and collective superpowers, but we also reject the notion that we have anything to do with genius. It feels delusional, self-aggrandizing, or just plainly egomaniacal. Nevertheless, I believe that each of us has the potential to discover, cultivate, and share with the world our own distinctive genius. Ultimately, groups have not only a collective superpower potential but also a collective genius waiting to be used and expanded.

My guess is that over 95 percent of all of us never get the chance to even discover the potential of our genius, let alone nurture it and share it with those around us and the rest of the world. Contrary to superpowers that can be used either constructively or destructively, genius is not only a synthesis of superpowers; it's also purposefully directed toward the benefit of others. You know that you are in your genius zone when you are not only benefiting from its expression but others are gaining too.[5]

Taking Others Seriously

A lot of the work in caring first aims to create a space to take seriously our own superpowers and genius and those of others. I suspect that one of the reasons that Marvel's comics are so popular is that they're explored often through their Justice League, the power of the collective effort. Even if you have superpowers, the influence that comes from assembling your force to those of others is unparalleled. It takes creative courage to care first because our usual and well-intentioned expectation from the start is to focus most of our energy toward other aims, such as discovering breakthroughs, collaboration, or growth.

How I Discovered My Genius

Words are powerful. They offer direction, guidance, and self-reflection. On a personal level, caring first means finding the words to offer guidance and self-reflection. My objective is not to reinvent the wheel. Many tools that already exist, like the famous StrengthsFinder and TTI Success Insights, are helpful and powerful in finding constructive words that can guide your process and thinking in extracting the superpowers and the genius from you and your team. They've helped me clarify and zoom in on some of the strengths I have and how to put them into action. With personal coaching as another support, I found profound inspiration and help in using words as a source of light for what I could offer the world.

Building Your Narrative

In the process of creating a new story, a live show, or a play, for example, soon enough you start working on inventing and establishing the conventions (rules) of that world you are trying to create. Depending on the story, in theater, you develop a set of rules to create a world—say, that these shoes are going to be magical or that this cane will fly. You give invented yet real properties to objects and characters. The more coherent and legitimate this world is, even if that world doesn't exist, the more easily it will find its audience and resonate deeply.

I think this is true for us as individuals but also for our companies and their cultures. Establishing the conventions of our personal worlds and the ones related to our organizations calls for crafting our narratives. Ultimately, though, I found that it's when you engage in your own creative process to build your personal narrative that even more resonant words emerge, defining for you and others what genius truly means. In other words, no matter what test, personality scan, or coaching support I've taken, I have found it tremendously helpful, inspiring, and relevant to craft my own words.

I found inspiration by discovering and working with so many outstanding talents who had developed an intimate relationship with their inner story, especially during my years working in film casting or while talent scouting at Cirque du Soleil. I grew up in an immigrant family of ambivalent seekers who had so much hope in my success. They left everything in the south behind to come up north, but were always uncertain of how to fit into this new world they had chosen for us. It was a source of great heartbreak for them and for me that I never finished college, as this was the pinnacle of the success they had in mind for me, which I had integrated unwittingly. Developing the storytelling skills that helped me recreate my own personal narrative, while also building upon the qualifiers from different tests, coaching support and experiences, proved invaluable in transforming the heartbreak of my perceived failures into something meaningful and powerful that can evolve over time. It gave me a chance to own my words fully and to add nuances that no machine, program, or the perceptions and hopes from loved ones can offer alone. It gave me an opportunity to develop my own intimate relationship with the value of my inner story.

Putting My Own Words on It

I've discovered that including others was something that drove me; I never felt good seeing people left behind. Growing up, I made sure that when I was the captain of a team, I picked early the kid who usually got picked last. Perhaps because of the war on imagination at home, the high level of invisible stress I was dealing with growing up, I excel today at creating and leading in contexts that are about pioneering work (building things almost from scratch with big challenges in front of us) or about redressing (saving the show when everything else broke loose).

To name a few things, I was deeply moved when I read *To Kill a Mockingbird* (fighting an unjust world) and *Between the World and Me* (revealing an unjust world); when I saw films as diverse as *House of Fog* and *Sandcast* (the immigrant father torn between his heritage and the one his son will have), *In America* (the hardship of immigration), and *Ratatouille* (the misfit that prevails against all odds); and, more recently, heard about the coverage of the *New York Times* on Canadian families who were hosting refugees from Syria in 2016. My emotional, inspired response to these stories offers a mirror and some wind to lift the fog, the mystery about my own genius. The pattern that keeps coming back to me is how moved I am by the underdog and the one who was told all his life that he couldn't make it, that he didn't have what it takes.

The way I translated this narrative into a genius was about creating the ideal, optimal, nurturing space for other people to shine and express their own genius. In that way, my work resembles that of a master gardener, nurturing a sequoia one hour and then attending to bonsai and rough bushes, all for the sake of expressing light and oxygen to create beauty and meaning. Who's your genius?

Elizabeth Gilbert suggests evocatively that our genius lives close to us, passing by from time to time on its own rhythm and schedule.[6] I suggest a slightly different view. I think that inside all of us sits a genius. It waits to be discovered, hoping that it can be cultivated and eventually shared. The practice of caring first ultimately means developing a fearless intimacy with that genius; it means becoming so good at listening to its potential that we can offer it to ourselves and the world. It's the first antidote to disengagement and the war on imagination. Finally, caring first is not about compromising the quality of the work or the standards of excellence that you have set for yourself and your business. It's about doing things with consideration for the thoughts, aspirations, and deep talents of the people that you are working with. Although popular culture suggests that you only have a choice between ruthlessness or kindness and corresponding results between success and middle-of-the-road results, I'm proposing the idea that you can hold people to very high standards of excellence while caring more broadly for who they are as humans. Caring first is not conditional on what you receive in return. It's a leadership decision you take to elevate yourself and your organization, wherever you are.

II. Insights

Practices

The following practices will help you develop caring first:

- *Listening.* This is the central practice of caring first for the team and for yourself. It simply involves listening actively, with intent to truly understand and act on what you understand. It's a practice that improves in quality when we use it often. As deceptively simple as it appears to be, mastering it requires some time. To capture as many thoughts about the aspirations and thinking of your team, it's best to think of formal, informal, and anonymous ways to capture what your team has in their heart and mind.

- *Informal connections.* Creating opportunities for people to connect informally, particularly people who don't know each other, offers a context conducive to sharing aspirations and dreams. One of the most powerful ways I have experienced in creating these informal yet powerful connections is through learning to cook food together with a chef. The evocative experience of learning to cook a meal together and then sharing that meal as a group is a beautiful metaphor to create these informal connections that can lead you to know more about your team's aspirations, values, hopes, and dreams.

- *The importance of saying thank you.* When we go fast or the war on imagination takes hold, we can forget the fundamentals, like having rituals of celebration to say thanks, and give credit to those who deserve it. Saying thank you is one of the simplest yet most powerful ways to show care. Not recognizing the accomplishments, big and small, by a team is one of the safest ways over time to contribute to the disengagement of your team.

- *Changing rituals and updating communications.* Be clear with your team about what you are changing when a ritual gets upgraded, changed, or canceled. If, for example, you celebrated your team's accomplishment with large posters at the main entrance of your headquarters, a tradition at Cirque du Soleil, and you suddenly stop doing that with no explanation, you're showing the opposite of care, even if it seems a small detail. Such situations risk creating the wrong story to tell about you and your organization.

- *Stealing credit is a short-term game.* Taking credit for what someone else on your team has done can be demoralizing. Instead, celebrate others' accomplishments.

- *High performance, competition, and pushing the limits.* What about competition and rivalry? If I care for people too much, isn't there a risk that they will get too comfortable, take advantage of me, and slack off? What about pushing people to their limit? What about high perform-ance? I argue that when you show care for people, you not only set the ground for high performance over time. It has the added benefit of revealing those who are not ready to receive your care. A more caring environment can even help you more easily identify team members and employees who are not a good fit for the culture to which you are contributing or that you are trying to create. In other words, by caring first we don't lower our standards for performance; in fact, we might discover along the way that those standards are enhanced.

- *People should do their jobs, right?* What about the risk of letting the genie out of the lamp? If we offer our team members, collaborators, and employees a chance to work with their superpowers and they start to think they have a genius of their own, who's going to do their jobs if they quickly find the work boring? Working with people's real potential should push you to work toward the best fit between superpowers and roles. If someone can't make the company benefit from its superpowers because there's no alignment between the two, then it's a miscast that should be corrected.

- *Coaching.* If you can, find a coach who is passionate about the growth of others. Not only will you benefit from the mirror this person will offer you, but this person can help you improve your own critical skills as a listener to yourself and to others. Encourage your team to do so too.

Exercises

Push your reflection, capture your reactions, make it personal:

- *Find, articulate, and write down your superpowers.* Think about the things that you truly love, are passionate about, and aspire to. When you join a project, enter a meeting room, attend a conference, what qualities, characteristics, and strengths do you put forward? What are the things that you excel at? You don't need to be the best in the world at it (remember you don't have to be a superhero to have superpowers). Have you done any online or in-person assessment, with or without a coach, that offers words and qualifiers that still resonate for you? Have fun with the concept. Maybe you have strong intuition, or maybe you can see through the numbers. What can you do that you are not already doing to nurture these superpowers? Assess how close you are to your superpowers. Are they constructive or destructive? How could you turn things around if some are destructive?

• *Listen for aspirations.* Pay attention and ask about your team members' aspirations. What are they dreaming about? What do they consider beautiful? What matters to them the most?

• *Practice daily internal listening.* What do you do regularly, even daily, to capture your thinking, reflections, and emotional experiences? Have you tried writing first thing in the morning for ten minutes? Do you meditate and then, at the end of the session, write your thoughts? Whatever you do, discover a practice that works for you and offers you a moment, as regularly as possible, to listen deeply to the experiences around you and what's happening inside you. Think of it as daily or regular hygiene and ultimately keep track of your evolving aspirations.

• *Find the collective superpower.* Map the superpowers of five people close to you. See if you can do the same with a small team you are working with on a project with right now. Ask all members individually what they think their superpower is at work and what they aspire to in the years to come at work and beyond. Map their responses on paper and add yours to the mix. See if you can also add the superpower of your organization. Risk using your intuition to label the collective superpower of the group. Do you need to align things more? Could you do more to nurture those superpowers?

• *Build your narrative with your own words.* First, assemble all the significant words from tests and assessments that stayed with you and still mean something to you. Write these down on a large sheet of paper without trying to organize them too much. Picture your piece of paper as a large net that's capturing all those technical words about you, collected over the years, assembled into one place. Then scan the last five years for events, art, sport, culture, music, and other experiences that truly moved you. Don't think too much about it; there's not a right or a wrong. This is an assessment to add words that are coming from you on top of technical words that are useful but perhaps less personal. List everything you consider memorable and deeply meaningful to you, from a great TV series to someone you met and a conference you went to that left you moved, changed, inspired. It can be deep, but it doesn't need to be; maybe it's something that you remember that made you laugh hard. Next, look at those words together and see if something emerges—a pattern, a theme, or something that you could start phrasing in a similar sentence to this: "My genius is about___for other people." Finally, let it sit for a few hours or days, revisiting as many times as you need. Use it as a guide and source of inspiration to frame your work and evaluate if you align or not with these aspirations that are inside your genius.

• *Draft or enhance the narrative of your organization.* In 1987, when Cirque du Soleil famously found success in Santa Monica, one could have said that the narrative of the company was "We are ready to lose everything to give everything." The legendary story that year tells the tale of a troupe having just enough resources to travel from Canada to Santa Monica, but not enough to get back if the tour was unsuccessful. That year, Cirque du Soleil's narrative resonated with its audience, and it was rewarded with acclaims that continue to this day. What's the narrative of your organization, business, or team? If you don't like it, what would the new one be? How could the superpowers in your team members help reach that renewed narrative?

• *Superimpose narratives and superpowers.* When you superimpose your narrative and your perceived narrative for your company, how much alignment and harmony do you account for? Do you get a similar picture or a different one when you superimpose your superpowers and the ones from your company or your team? What can you learn from either the lack of alignment or the presence of alignment?

• *Use the power of symbols.* Find an object that can represent your top superpower and that you can bring with you to work.

• *Use the power of collective symbols.* Ask your team members to bring to work an object that represents for them one of their most important superpowers. Do this in a meeting or individual session. It can be a great ice-breaker to have a conversation about aspirations and dreams and how to leverage superpowers more inside work.

• *Build a wall of fame.* Can you build of wall of fame for all the superpowers on your team? Can you be inspired by what superheroes do with their talisman? How could you feature those objects as a reminder of the collective superpowers of your group? What other ideas could you use to leverage the symbolic and visual potential around the superpowers that superheroes are so good at showcasing?

• *Draw the shape of your genius.* When you put all your main superpowers together and think about something that can benefit the world around you, what shape, name, or form does it give your genius? What can you do to discover more about it? How can you develop it more? How will you share it more at work?

• *What if you map the main superpowers and genius of your audience, clients, customers, and fans?* What would that be if you were to map the seven strongest? How would you aggregate it? Would that influence the current understanding of your brand?

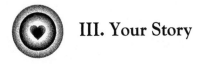 ## III. Your Story

Summary

The war on imagination takes many expressions. One of the most devastating ways it manifests itself at work is through disengagement. People become negative and cynical, productivity is affected, innovation slows or stops, and clients and customers typically start to feel the negativity as well.

We have a natural tendency to think that respect needs to be reinstituted for engagement to happen again, but that's a false answer. Although respect is important, caring comes before it. Caring first is the initial stage along the way to greater, stronger, and more meaningful innovation. Caring first is like deposits in a bank account with an unusually high interest rate, except there's no hoax or pyramid scheme. As you practice to make deposits, even small ones, like listening to a colleague's deep or superficial aspirations, safety, and eventually trust, set in. From that trust, respect emerges, always fragile and potentially stronger when nurtured.

There's nothing particularly original in saying that we have inside us aspirations, superpowers, and a distinctive genius waiting to grow and touch the world. But I believe that inside our families, businesses, projects, companies, and organizations, there are also collective superpowers and a collective genius too often ignored or unknown. Most of the time, that genius and those superpowers are left dormant or not maximized.

In caring first, we do our best to celebrate those. Caring first's most powerful and simple tool is listening for the aspirations, superpowers, and eventually genius inside all of us and our teams. When you care about the aspirations of your team members, you can leverage those aspirations, dreams, and superpowers for the benefit of your employees and your organization. When you do that, you are already living through genius.

Although the concept of superpowers is not new, what has been overlooked is the idea that when you bring your entire team together, there's also an opportunity to awake the collective superpower of your group and therefore its collective genius. We think at times that we have a problem with respect, but in fact we need to cultivate the creative courage to care before anything else.

Checklist

- What are the services used (such as at the gym, hotel, airlines, school, and other organizations) where I experienced some of the best examples of caring first or some of the most neglectful practices? Draw examples from the big picture or about details.

- How much do I know about my employees' deep and superficial aspirations?

- Have I set up formal, informal, and anonymous approaches and devices to capture what's in my team members' hearts and minds?

- Do I have practices that reflect what I hear and what I understand to make sure that I'm getting it right?

- How much do I know about my own aspirations and dreams? Do I take them seriously?

- What's the common ground between the genius of my business, of myself, and of my employees? If I work on my own or with collaborators, am I in harmony with the genius of my business and my own genius? In all scenarios, is there common ground? Does realizing this or becoming more conscious about it change something in the way I will conduct my business and project?

CHAPTER 3

Secure Safety

No Safety, No Trust

Do not fear mistakes. There are none.

Miles Davis[1]

I. Raising the Curtain

The show is about to begin. From where we are, the smell of incense and water is unescapable yet never overpowering. It calls for ritual and concentration despite the laughter we hear afar. I'm not in my seat yet but standing, about 110 feet in the air, on a metal floor through which I can see everything below, giving me more a sense of suspension than support. Three colleagues from the O show company[2] in Las Vegas are with me. An acrobatic coach, a rigging technician, and the trapeze artist are getting ready to fly below. From high above, I can see the seats, in miniature, and the audience, walking to their seats, both half alert and half relaxed as they wait for the magic to begin imminently. I love those moments of preparation.

Other than the glow from the theater below and the meticulous and cautious blue light from the technician's small flashlight focusing on the artist's security, you could barely hear yourself think from the obscurity and the impressive height. When the light faded and the music started, the Las Vegas audience, known for its rowdy, noisy ways, stilled. Above, the artist sat calmly, helped by the technician, close to the edge of the metal grid (by the look on her face, you'd never guess that we were standing so high) where an opening welcomed her as she began her slow descent, half falling, half flying, over the audience. For the few minutes before she made her way through that opening in the grid, I stood there quietly, admiring the silent communication between her, the rigging technician, and her coach. How could she appear so calm, so high? How could she have built so much trust in her team and herself? Safety is at a premium when you are so high in the air. In less than two minutes, in character, she would join the audience as we stayed up a few more moments. Enigmatic and mysterious, she announced by her mere presence the beginning of a world of wonder. It was an inspiring aerial ballet, but also puzzling to see the rigor and beauty of their attentive choreography of ropes, carabiners, and double-checks. It's that dance, revisited and perfected hundreds of times, that made the fabric of the artists' safety protocol.

In pure contrast, an experience I had had along with several employees and partners at Cirque du Soleil was to jump in a foam pit containing about 25,000 foam cubes. The process is simple: I was pulled with a rope by a technician using a pulley system over the pit to a cradle station roughly thirty feet above the pit. With my harness still on, I stood up on the small platform and jumped. What seemed modest from the floor quickly became a source of panic and cold sweat once I was on the platform, and it took me a few minutes to finally jump over the obstacles in my head. Eventually the better understanding of the security around the jump I was about to make made me act on my commitment.

An old proverb proposes compellingly to jump or leap to make the net appear. Although I love its poetry and invitation to faith, when I consider what we need to create the best context for innovation to happen and to push back the war on imagination, I would rephrase the proverb: "To jump to greater heights and contain the many mistakes you will make along the way, you need to see the net. Jump to greater heights when you see the net." After you have established caring first, securing safety is the most important and concrete action you can take on your way to a more collaborative, innovative, and creative workplace.

In Search of Innovation with the Body

Over the past two decades, part of my work has been to help search for the potential of the human body to amaze. From scouting talents in India, Amsterdam, New York, Johannesburg, and many more cities, I benefited from discussions and exchanges with some of the world's leading experts in high-flying performances, circus acrobatics, dance, music, and the performing arts. I searched everywhere for new, unexpected ways for the body to move and amaze an audience.

In my experience working with hundreds of artists and managers across disciplines, I realized that a serious path to creating great work starts with caring first through securing safety for the artists and managers. The search for those incredible moments of magic to happen onstage is usually anchored in our ability to create a great safety net (literal and metaphorical) that provides space for mistakes to happen. Without that safety, movement and meaning don't coalesce as much to create moments of pure surprise, pure electricity, and genuine emotions.

If the importance of securing safety when you are trying to create and innovate at 110 feet above the ground is compelling and, moreover, if securing safety is also relevant for dancers (e.g., providing the best floors possible, developing a good warm-up and routine schedule), musicians (preventative physiotherapy), and other artistic and sports disciplines, it might not always be that clear in the context of other kinds of work. My argument is to bring to the forefront that the extension of caring first in our businesses, companies, and generally at work is to secure safety. This is another crucial stage toward creating and producing work that people will remember for the right reasons because it will have created value in their lives.

The Importance of Securing Safety

Why is securing safety so important beyond the obvious protection of life? The war on imagination prevents you from accepting your vulnerabilities and forces you to pretend that they are not there while still disempowering you. It wants you to delegate your agency to someone else who will decide for you. But to create something compelling that will resonate with others, even if your work is designing life insurance packages, you need to insert some of your vulnerabilities in the process of putting it all together. You need to offer something real that people can relate to. To be vulnerable here means that you accept that your path toward meaningful, important innovation and resonance will include mistakes, failures, and fears alongside wins, successes, and praise. It also means that you can use some of those vulnerabilities to make your work stronger, more relatable, and more human and, in return, more resonant and valuable for others.

A Net for Higher Standards

During the creation of a show, nets, mattresses, safety ropes, and myriad other security devices or protocols are installed to protect the cast and crew. It's safety that's demonstrated concretely: everyone can see and feel it around them, and it aims to keep everyone away from harm.

In a context where you are trying to create something new and resonant—in short, when you are trying to innovate—that safety not only protects your team; it also creates a physical space that allows them to open up to their vulnerability. You need that vulnerability to create something original yet universal. In the perspective of live performance, you install a net to protect people while they are trying to push the limits and come up with something never seen before. As they attempt to reach a new level of performance, they will make mistakes and miscalculations; that secured safety will offer them the assurance of limiting the negative impact of those mistakes.

Beyond the physical protection and the invitation to be vulnerable to discover something new, the net offers a third message, subtle but probably the most powerful: extraordinary work can be achieved because of that protection. The net suggests that higher standards and breakthroughs are possible through exploration, risk taking, and sound safety.

Precarious Situations

It's possible to create and innovate in any context. The most difficult context to create and innovate in happens when an organization doesn't live up to its potential to go further, or a business succumbs under the weight of the war on imagination without even realizing and missing a chance to fight back. You can create under the gun, under duress, and even under extreme danger; the history of art, and indeed our entire human history, abounds with examples of masterpieces and break-throughs that occurred in extreme situations. I'd argue, though, that this is not a sustainable situation from the viewpoint of collaborative, collective work. The outcome of the work becomes something not only unpredictable but ultimately negative for you, your colleagues, your business, and the people you serve through it.

Securing safety offers a chance for everyone to work in a spirit of excellence without compromising high standards while recognizing that to create outstanding work, you will expose yourself and your team to being vulnerable because you will make mistakes. If your environment doesn't concretely support and secure safety around mistakes and the discovery process, the normal progression of innovation that includes overcoming fears, doubts, and uncertainty stalls or becomes destructive.

Determining How Safe Your Organization Is

How do we reconcile the desire to reach the highest level of performance, accomplishments, and innovation with the underlying message of making sure that we secure safety within our teams? How can it be okay to fall, miss the movement, make a mistake in an environment that's visually or physically benevolent? What about the idea of no gain without pain? What about the idea of the terrorizing coach dictating brutally the road to winning the championship?

Being passionate not only about the outcome but also about the quality and growth quality of the process, I believe that most of these stereotypical approaches damage the actors over the long term, staining in the process the history of the accomplishment once people look back on it. Because suffering inevitably comes with more suffering, I think that the suffering is more meaningful when supported by an environment that's safe. When that suffering is meaningful because we know that there's room for the inevitable mistakes and failures, the next stage, fostering trust, becomes accessible. In other words, you can achieve great heights without focusing on securing safety for your team, preferring perhaps to manipulate, control, and pit people against each other. But the best you can foster then is blind loyalty, not trust. Down the line, the implication that this has for your aspirations to innovate can be important. The risk is for your team, clients and customers to feel a lack of generosity coming out of your offerings, your services and your work without them necessarily being able to articulate their negative impressions about that work.

In its most successful manifestation, securing safety is as clear as a net over a stage and as limpid as the rope that helps the artist to climb. It's not so much about what you say but what you and your environment demonstrate. If there is no net, vulnerabilities are all over the place, unchecked, uncontained, and uncontrolled. Whatever you do in such a context is affected negatively. And finally, even with the net, there is enough space and air through it to favor exploration and circulation of ideas while protecting. A few questions are useful in helping you determine whether your organization is safe:

- How clear is the path to growing inside the organization for a newcomer?
- Is human resources (HR) seen as objective or partial to top leadership?
- Are there truly anonymous ways to send feedback, thoughts, questions, and recommendations straight to the top?
- Is there feedback that comes from that anonymous feedback?
- Do you feel that you have more or less of a influence on the growth of your organization?

- Is it okay for leaders and other powerful individuals within the organization to talk down to same-level colleagues and less influential colleagues? Have you ever witnessed such a situation? If so, how did you feel about? How is it justified?

- Is it acceptable for some members of your organization to behave in disrespectful ways because of their status, role, beliefs, and stereotypes (e.g., "artists are temperamental," "CEOs have high-pressure jobs that make them impatient")?

- When there's an issue regarding the physical or psychological safety of employees around you, how clear is it what to do next?

- Is credit offered to those to whom it is due?

- What is the ratio of communication between the top people in your organization and the bottom: 90 percent to 10 percent? The opposite? Somewhere in the middle? Something else?

- Is there a monopoly on who can come up with ideas and original and creative thinking?

- How integrated or in silos are members of your teams, departments, and divisions?

- Is the culture of your workplace supportive of diversity of ages, gender, academic background, disciplines, ethnicity, and so on? If so, are team members diverse? How can you create a more unexpected mix of people with diverse backgrounds and disciplines?

- How safe do you feel to make mistakes?

- In your opinion, does leadership understand its process of innovation? Is that process clear to most people in the company?

- If you are part of formal leadership, do you feel that you have a good grasp of the innovation cycle at your company, with its pitfalls and glories?

- How inclusive do you consider the culture of your company, particularly regarding nonconventional profiles, minorities, women, younger employees, and other profiles that may contrast with the establishment of your organization?

- Has there been bullying, harassment, or even outright violence in your company? Was it dealt with skillfully in your opinion?

- Are programs, policies, and approaches updated, communicated, and understood when it comes to bullying, harassment, and violence? Do you understand them? Are the programs, policies, and approaches simple or complex? Are people serious or lax about them?

- What are the most potent direct dangers for your employees and teams in their organizational role? What ways to prevent them are in place? How clear are those strategies?

- Must you choose between safety and artistry? Structure and creativity? Finance and art? Business and production? Business and everything else?

- What if your business was a political system? Is it a monarchy? Street gang? Parliamentarian? Dictatorship? Benevolent authority? Commune? Tribal? Something else?

- What percentage of people in your business, according to your opinion, feel included and respected when they show up at the table? What's your intuitive response?

These are just a few examples to help point toward what shape your net could take when you are evaluating how to better secure safety in your organization. Securing safety means contributing to an environment where people can clearly see markers of protection if something goes wrong and mistakes are made as a sign that you care for them and as a reminder that you are all working together to do extraordinary things. The key word related to securing safety is *clarity*, and it's an extension of caring first. Finally, it supports practicing at a higher altitude for you and your organization.

How to Create or Reinforce Your Virtual Net

Securing safety is about creating or reinforcing the virtual net inside your organization that will support your team members when you encourage them to venture out of the box to help discover the next well of value for your business or your organization. The questions just listed offer you an initial scan of weak areas or areas that might benefit from greater clarity. Every organization will have its own reality to factor into securing safety. Section II identifies some areas that might help support and organize your reflection.

II. Insights

Practices

Create a Safe Environment

Generally a culture of inclusion does wonders to create safety, whereas secrecy and exclusiveness tend to erode the sense of safety and negate attempts to establish trust, let alone build on it. Public space that promotes the circulation and the informal connection of people is an efficient way to secure safety. Whether at Cirque du Soleil or at companies with a large, varied age spectrum, the kitchen has been positioned as a hub for people to connect, and it works pretty well. IDEO San Francisco, for example, organizes a tea ritual around its kitchen, and Disney in Burbank has a tree of wishes set along the path to the kitchen as an example of how the environment can participate in securing safety.

Choose Words That Create Harmony

Words are receptacles of meaning. Each has a different texture that helps point to a different concept or story. Their surface can shine when our intention and their meaning are in harmony. They can unintentionally create a distortion when intention and meaning are not in harmony.

A longtime tradition at Cirque du Soleil is what we call lion's den. It refers to a critical session between a creation team and the creative guide of the company and its top executives. For more than two decades, Cirque's founder, Guy Laliberté, presided over these sessions, which were reputed to be ruthless and blunt for the creative team. The goal of these sessions, though, is not so much to create fear or frustrations as to provide a space for candid, honest feedback on the work's progression.

When I led the creation of *MJ ONE*, I proposed that we call these important sessions with Guy and the rest of the executive team "jam" (referring to one of Michael's songs) rather than "lion's den." The expression "lion's den" proposes a powerful image, although its more profound meaning didn't confer the image I wanted to offer my team for this project. After all, people are usually thrown in the lion's den to be devoured, and that was not going to be true in my case.

Be mindful of the words you use for your most critical (and not so critical) sessions, meetings, and conferences. At times, traditions or the impact of the war on imagination prevent us from thinking clearly about what makes sense at this moment. It's not about desecrating the celebrated traditions of your company, however old they are, but about questioning if the words you use when you meet with and give roles to people and label projects support safety.

Keep Everyone Informed

Informing your partners early can sometimes be the best way to secure safety and build a foundation for trust. Find out who prefers to be informed early even if the information is incomplete. Then strike a balance that allows you to keep your team and partners in the loop and away from last-minute information that makes them feel like an adversary to your objectives.

Be Both Real and Kind

I lost count of the number of auditions I've led, meetings where I had bad news to deliver, sessions with artists I had to offer feedback to after a lackluster performance or about issues off the stage. I'm perplexed that culture offers us a choice between being real with people or being kind, which is a caricature that doesn't reflect every reality. I believe in direct feedback when things go well *and* when they don't.

Over the years, I've delivered hard news about artists not selected during an audition and colleagues who needed support during a rough patch or whom I needed to let go, and I always did my best to be both kind and real. In debates over creative decisions to figure out, creators to choose, or tough choices to make, I advocated for being real and kind with people. Although it takes creative courage to practice and apply it, I believe that it's accessible to all of us. It's okay to rise above the clichés of the intransigent leader and the one full of heart who is unable to say anything negative to people.

Develop Diverse Workforces

If you send a marine engineer, a film director, a teacher, and a pastor into a forest with instructions to come back in one hour with something from that forest that reminds them of their childhood, chances are that they will come back with very different things and certainly with different stories about those objects.

Part of the success of an organization that wants to expand its innovation effort, its collaborative capacity, and its talent at imagining the future resides in the diversity of the people at its table. When I refer to diversity, I mean people who are different in many ways; they don't all come from the same college, aren't the same age, and have different backgrounds, places of origin, genders, disciplines, and interests.

One of the reasons for Cirque du Soleil's success has been its ability to bring together artists and disciplines that break the orthodoxy of what a circus is thought to be. It brings together people who typically don't work together, on and off stage, to create something that hasn't been seen before. Managing and leading diversity is hard. You must integrate a higher set of aspirations, but that also means that you might benefit from an unexpected mix of superpowers and geniuses that is just right for your organization.

Finally, diverse space taking into consideration the need for areas optimal for introversion and extroversion, and both formal and sporadic meetings can do wonders to help create more safety. Thinking about your space with these elements in mind can facilitate securing safety for everyone inside your organization since it tends to be more supportive of misfits—the odd man out or odd woman out who could make the next important difference in your business.

Practice an Open Table Approach

Practice having an open table approach and an open door or preserve the ones you do have. During a painful divorce process and while I was in charge of the creative direction of several projects for the media department, I started to shut my door. I was also shutting down inside; I didn't want to share my personal difficulties with my team and instead preserved a professional stance with everyone at work.

After two months of trying to keep to myself, I faced a revolt from my small team and superior, who didn't recognize me anymore. I thought that I was doing the right thing by not sharing my situation and reducing my accessibility during a touchy period for me. They were asking me to instead feel safe by becoming real with them.

In that same spirit, reflecting on how easy or not real feedback can make it to the top of our organization, whether it rains or not, is equally important. What saved me back then was that I valued the feedback and benefited from their efforts to talk to me.

Offer Options for Collective and Solitary Space

In open plan offices, it's vital to offer options for people to isolate themselves for more concentration or simply for a respite. This alone can secure safety in any work context. I share a few general ideas about my ideal design principle for work in Chapter 6.

Exercises

The following exercises will help you secure safety:

- If you answered the questions at the end of Section I, draw a map of the two main areas of intervention where securing more safety for you, your staff, or your team. Might that exercise help support greater collaboration and stronger innovation initiatives?

- What do you need to feel safer in your role? How would you go about securing more safety for you and your colleagues? Who could be your partner in such a project? What two or three specific objectives around securing safety would you have in mind?

- Who will share your voice if you don't? Did you know that the most interesting thing about you is *you*? What would be on your list of the most interesting things about you? If you think about a colleague you appreciate, what would your list of his or her attributes be? What about a colleague you have some difficulty collaborating with? What are some of the interesting, valuable attributes of that person that you could isolate? Can this be an opportunity to find common ground with him or her?

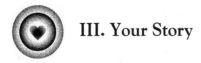

III. Your Story

Summary

We are not securing safety just for the sake of it, just because it's nice and humane to do so, although this alone would be a good reason. We want to secure safety because to accomplish extraordinary things and create incredible products, memorable services, and outstanding experiences, we have a better chance of reaching for the stars when a safety net protects us and our team. Obstacles and failures, big and small, are inevitable along the way to great achievements, so setting a net is smart. Pushing innovation and brand relevance further takes creative courage, guts, and practice knowing that every time we jump, the net will be there. We won't be let down.

Securing safety has a number of benefits:

- It puts in place visible, concrete devices, tools, and protocols that act like a virtual net. That net protects and helps people push their limits because they feel safe to be vulnerable in their pursuit of excellence.
- It helps to defend your team against harm, physical and psychological, and from the danger that comes with leading, changing, and transforming aspects of the world.
- It helps you see mistakes, fears, and doubts as part of most innovation processes rather than as anomalies to eradicate or hide.
- It's an invitation to everyone in the organization to walk with creative courage toward trust because of the power of caring first and its extension in securing safety.

When we care first and, by extension, secure safety, respect emerges naturally. And when we foster enough trust, respect becomes an expression of appreciation. Here are a few examples of ways to help secure safety at work, evidence that a net of safety was installed:

- An HR manager reminds a worker of the absolute confidentiality of the session before a meeting starts.

- A workshop on what to do in the case of harassment, how to recognize it, and who to reach out to shows genuine care.

- An anonymous way for team members to send real and honest feedback provides a fundamental door to the soul of your organization and to your team. It shows that there is space for improvement coming from anywhere inside the organization. It's hard work because you need to acknowledge the input but it's also a great extension of caring first for your audience, inside and out of your organization.

- An equitable and fair approach to pay that transcends gender, country of origin, and age sends the message that equity and fairness (supreme indicators of safety) are at the top of your preoccupations and something that you take seriously. Most of us are familiar with these issues around equity and fairness; nonetheless, the reality around equity shows that most organizations struggle to integrate these principles at the core of their mission.

- A smart organizational adjustment helps to blend parts of our personal and professional life at work thanks to technology.

Checklist

- Do you need to put protocols in place to secure aspects of your workplace that need attention?

- How can you secure more safe places in your personal practice? Do you have a "refuge," a safe place of your own to do deep work, to reflect, to manage crises, to retreat and bring clarity to your work? If you don't have one, how would you go about designing a place of your own? What would your Batcave look and feel like? Why not sketch out a few silly ideas?

- Remember that words matter immensely. Should you update, or suggest updating, meeting names, conferences, and events that don't fully explain your intentions, ideas, and plans? Moreover, could you have unintentionally sent a message of danger to your team through some of the gatherings that you participate in, organize, or design?

CHAPTER 4

Foster Trust

The Natural State of Silos

The best way to find out if you can trust somebody is to trust them.

Ernest Hemingway[1]

I. Raising the Curtain

Trust

When we care for people's creative potential and secure their safety, respect emerges and trust is ripe, ready to grow. And when we show care for our own aspirations and our physical and psychological safety, we help create conditions to foster trust in ourselves and make it more difficult for the war on imagination to grasp at us. It makes us better leaders and improves the outcomes of our efforts toward innovation and breakthroughs.

Trust finds its strongest anchor in collaboration. In the best cases of constructive collaboration, we create something together that would be difficult or impossible to do on our own. That accomplishment makes all parties proud. Because we feel seen, safe, and accepted for our gifts and our vulnerabilities, we naturally foster trust to create something that meets a new challenge. Remember that trust is a fragile, dynamic, powerful process. It can be broken during the collaboration cycle as much as it can be reinforced.

Good Intentions, Wrong Results

At times, we might be puzzled by the results of our initiatives. We might feel, for example, that we have demonstrated care and secured safety, only to find the symptoms of the war on imagination raging with mistrust stronger than ever.

My parents deeply cared for me, but the way they cared was through unrelentingly worrying about me. They warned me about dangers in the world and tried to shield me as much as they could from exposure to that world. But as they did this, they weren't succeeding in helping me feel seen, considered, and respected for who I was. There was no space for my aspirations, and I stopped believing that I had potential. The more care they wanted to show, the less I felt respected because they didn't realize that they were confusing care and worry. And the more they wanted to enforce safety, the less I felt considered because there was no space for trust and therefore collaborations to happen between us. Perhaps this lack of recognition explains why as I was growing up, I developed a passion and love for meeting new challenges that involve improving relationships and the organizational cultures around them.

A New Role

I am always excited when I am offered a chance to help solve a new problem, crack a difficult code, or rise above a new challenge. Around 2005, Cirque du Soleil was growing exponentially, and the opportunities to obtain more responsibilities were too. The number of new shows to create and the different needs of the shows already deployed were adding pressure on our internal casting department and putting all of us in the spotlight. I had already been on the road for more than six years, traveling the world, searching for unique, generous, and extraordinary artists, performers, and talents when I was offered leadership of a small team of casting advisors who would work and service the artistic directors of the different shows.

Artistic directors were one of the primary clients of our team. They had the challenging job of being on the front line and taking care of the daily artistic needs of the show through the inevitable ups and downs. Although all of these artistic directors were different, they all had a demonstrated reputation for fierceness and a lack of patience. I think that in part, this was reflective of a general leadership style at Cirque that started at the top. Fierceness and lack of patience were indirectly encouraged.

When these directors stopped in Montreal to see recorded performances of the candidates, time was short, and we needed to be ready for them. Their mission was to keep the quality and the integrity of the show high, not an easy thing to do when they were responsible for anywhere from 320 to 470 shows every year, and they brought a lot of necessary fire into playing that role. Before YouTube became ubiquitous, my talent scout colleagues and I spent hours, sometimes through the night into the early morning, looking at thousands of VHS tapes, DVDs, even a few CD-ROMs from around the world. We then spent countless hours writing our evaluations in a massive electronic database with words and expressions like *great presence, would be perfect for this character,* or *second part funnier, maybe for a new creation? keep in file, riveting performance, stunning artistry.* Next came even more time selecting and presenting our potential candidates, from the expected jaw-dropping contortionist in Mongolia, to a dancer from Los Angeles, and a clown, that is, a physical actor, from Germany.

In my sixteen years at Cirque du Soleil, not one day was ever the same. Every talent scout had his or her own way of selecting and presenting candidates for an artistic director to review? Some would show, say, twelve candidates for a position where I might have presented three, and vice versa. The process was costly and time sensitive, and we had to find ways to cast as efficiently as possible and keep our operations sound.

My new mission was to help concentrate the tasks and responsibilities of casting advising in the hands of fewer talent scouts, who were now casting advisors, allowing the rest of the group to keep exploring the world for fresh new talent. I had to influence our work culture and organizational behaviors in a fast-paced environment of growth and wild, expanding success. I felt empowered, inspired, and fired up. I had great relational skills. I knew by heart the details of all the roles and characters on the nine existing shows, and I was enthusiastic about working with the artistic directors. I already saw how we could improve things, and I had a plan ready to go that would be truly helpful to all of us. But leading means exposing yourself to danger through either managing or influencing change.[2] I was trying to do both, and on my own.

I did everything I could to make things right by following experts' advice. I read about the importance of communication to build trust through clarity and creating a compelling offer for the new services of the casting advising team, and I had a talented team. That, however, didn't save my work from being an epic failure.

Very quickly I started to notice major resistance from the artistic directors—from those who were on the road and had little time to meet me while in Montreal to those in Las Vegas or Orlando who spent their time between Montreal and their show location. After a few months, I felt irrelevant in my role: most of the artistic directors had bypassed me to get to what they needed—fast access to the artists to cast. They didn't want to change things.

I was hurt and felt the bruise of being disregarded. I was revisiting the landscape of my childhood with the war on imagination raging and limiting my visual field.

I had been envisioning a fast, painless race to implementation but instead met with the perils of collaboration and the risks that come with any attempts to lead change in the world.

You might see some similarities with situations that you've experienced when you tried to change the status quo and transform your surrounding world. As I look back on this episode of my professional career, I see how several misconceptions contributed to failings in the critical stage of fostering trust with my artistic director partners.[3]

 ## II. Insights

The Path to Trust: Better Collaborations

How do we make things happen collectively? How do we work with people who have completely different, even divergent views on what's most important and needs to be done as priority? I've noticed in myself a set of false beliefs that were stopping me from creating deeper and more meaningful collaborative efforts. Those false beliefs are particularly persistent when we belong to a community. Because we have shared interests (the well-being of the company for example), we can assume, as I often did, that by nature, collaboration is inherent to the group. Of course, everywhere we look in our world, we see that collaborating is never as easy or as natural as it seems. This is true inside sports teams wearing the same jersey and sharing the simple goal of winning a game as it is true of fierce enemies on the world stage of international relations. Nonetheless, rising beyond the following three false beliefs can help us forge strong, collaborative teams and projects. And as hard as fostering trust to collaborate can be, I had an epiphany that it could also be simpler than I realized.

False Belief 1: Communities of Interest Are Collaborative, Naturally

My first major error was to assume that because we were part of a collective, that we formed a community, the "Cirque du Soleil team," we were collaborative by default, naturally. I didn't realize then that collaboration happens by design, through intent and creative construction. I had falsely merged team and teamwork, community and collective work, colleagues and collaboration as one and the same.

In team sports, we can see when a team is in a flow of collaboration and winning or whether infighting plagues its performance despite having top talent. When you listen to analyses of how well the team played, you will essentially hear how well they collaborated and fostered trust (or did not) in their group. You might also hear fans make the same mistake I did: thinking that it's an anomaly if the team wasn't being collaborative. Separating the activity of collaboration from being in a collective in a team or a group helps foster trust.

When people didn't collaborate, I felt the sting of the rejection personally as if I was in a schoolyard playing tag alone, away from the other kids. I found myself complaining that we were working too much in silos and I wished things were different. I was discovering that we were working in silos by nature and necessity and that fostering trust was the start of designing a collaborative context for work and innovation. I had to get two false beliefs out of the way and have one epiphany to start fostering trust.

False Belief 2: Authority Is Like Influence

That I was also confusing authority and influence prevented me even more from fostering trust with my partners rather than enforcing again and again my bestowed authority. As a new director, I looked at my environment from an organizational chart point of view. I wasn't considering how I was stepping into an established culture with people I needed to show care for first and secure safety for before proposing something new. Everybody agreed on the problems at hand, but we didn't take the time to agree on the way to address them collaboratively and I missed the opportunity to lead that specific work.

This confusion between authority and influence is a common mistake that we can observe at the highest levels of power by both novices and pros. In fact, authority and power work together: the more you have of each, the more leverage you potentially have as well. As we know, leverage is always limited, but power is finite.

False Belief 3: You Can Solve Collective Problems Alone

As much as I praised collaborative work back then, the truth is that I wanted to shine. I wanted to prove to those who had promoted me that they had made the right decision. In addition, working in silos at first facilitates things by speeding up the process of work. No hard work is required to build or foster trust with anyone else. But this silo bliss made it harder for the artistic directors to feel kinship with the project I was proposing. Finally, by working in a silo by myself, I was limiting their accountability if the initiative didn't work and therefore limiting their exposure to eventual problems. These were all ideal conditions for the war on imagination to surge and for the voice of doubt to spill over in me.

My Epiphany

I remember walking along the halls of the second floor of Cirque du Soleil's headquarters in Montreal when suddenly I recognized for the first time a simple idea that I'd never had before: every time that I was complaining or expressing my discontent to colleagues about how I thought that we should be a more collaborative group and that we worked too much in silos, I was contributing to the problem. That is when I started imagining that my mission was to create a bridge for people to collaborate by fostering trust.

I started with the assumption that maybe I was the only one at Cirque willing to collaborate and then saw that many others throughout the organization had the same interest, but were also too busy being sad about the situation to change something. This realization didn't change things instantly, yet it offered powerful insight into the importance of fostering trust and the possibilities of true collaborative work.

The hard work behind fostering trust helps create better collaborations. I realized that there was nothing automatic about collaboration and trust, even in a group that ultimately shared common objectives, and that I didn't need to take it personally and fall into the trap of the war on imagination. Eventually a question even emerged: What if our fear, inability, or difficulty in creating powerful collaborations and sustaining collaborative context beyond silos was in fact the outcome of a lack of imagination? And what if there was a link between this lack of imagination and a lack of compassion? If we have more compassion for our failings and those of our colleagues, can we have more trust for the work that we are trying to accomplish together?

A New Attitude

The decision that had the most influence on my development as a creative leader was to understand that I was the initiator of working toward trust and collaboration. It made me ask simple questions like: *What if I could get out of victimhood by simply deciding not to be a victim anymore? What if instead of lamenting the lack of collaboration in my group, I started doing something about it instead of waiting for someone else to initiate the effort?* Sometimes saying to ourselves "I'm the victim here" is the most comforting affirmation, on par with the negativity that the war on imagination triggers. It prevents us from asking another question, one that is scarier: *If I'm not the victim, what's left, and what's next?* What's hidden in plain sight is that by caring first, and securing more safety for ourselves and others, we foster trust without realizing it. And we discover that many others are also yearning to contribute to great, meaningful work that they couldn't accomplish on their own. When we wait for that trigger to come from someone else, we risk missing the opportunity to lead.

I started to see my role with a refreshed, renewed trust in my work and the platform it offered. Fostering trust meant trusting that I could play a role in improving what was a source of frustration, a lack of collaboration in our creative work, without having to change everything or wait for change to come from the top. That trust gave me the courage to reach out to others and discover that others shared my yearnings. We could create from our common ground, even when it seems almost impossible.

Collaboration can't work if it's only transactional. Although this is a radical idea, it also needs to be a gift, an act of personal leadership that says yes to others even if they appear to say no, initially, to our efforts.

Offering Trust or Expecting It

One way to look at the practice of fostering trust is to see it as something that we offer rather than as a transactional, conditional way of working. In other words, we become designers of a dynamic, volatile, active solution to foster trust without expecting anything more than not to add to the battle and the war on imagination. Our position becomes to either bring visionary collaborative skills to an environment where there's a deficiency or to add to the collaborative power when the culture where we work already encourages it. We become active at fostering trust by offering it and by creating a context where it can continue to grow or exposing a toxic environment that might decide to leave. The implication behind that approach is radical since it points to you as the first beneficiary of fostering trust. You foster trust because you will be the first to benefit, even if you are the only one that decides to join in. And if that trust is broken, you see it clearly. It's not about advocating naivety but about changing our mind-set toward actively building trust, creatively, humanly.

Why We Should Collaborate

Examples abound in the news and in publications about businesses, organizations, and systems that failed to create enough trust between their departments and in small and big groups. Often this failure to foster trust and the resulting defective collaborations led to catastrophic consequences, including death and billion-dollar fines. But behind these high-profile cases covered by mainstream media, many other organizations, and the people they serve, suffer and receive subpar services, products, and experiences precisely because trust hasn't been fostered, making collaborative effort that much more difficult.

Trust or Competition?

Do we have to choose between a highly competitive work environment where trust is a chimera or a place where trust expands steadily despite the highs and lows of the organization? Is there a contradiction between performance and compassion? Success and empathy? In my opinion and in my experience, we shouldn't have to choose. We have to foster trust while still having a highly competitive workforce able to accomplish what's perceived as impossible. As leaders, one way to achieve this is by playing the crucial role of reminding members of the team that the project they are working on is not about them. The project or mission is beyond them; it transcends them by channeling the goals of the project with the personal aspirations, superpowers, and genius at hand. When we have worked toward clarifying people's aspirations, superpowers, and genius, we can more easily help channel the work with a team that is supremely invested in the company's projects while having their own aspirations seen, respected, and less likely to take over the broader objectives. The glue to that approach is the ability to foster trust with yourself, your team, and the people that you are ultimately serving.

The Undiscussed Part of Innovation Work: Emotional Work

In the pursuit of innovation, imagination and creativity, the more you can trust your own vulnerabilities and doubts, the more you give yourself a chance to discover something that others can relate to. We fail to realize how much innovation work is emotional work. It's work that involves becoming fearless when looking at our own failings and worries, and giving to the work that we do a human texture and an emotional quality.

Practices

The following practices will help you foster trust.

Ask Dumb Questions!

If we are not ready to show our own vulnerabilities, we don't have the legitimacy to ask others to do so. I always let my teams know that one of my roles, when I participate in sessions, brainstorming, and other meetings that have ideation, problem solving and innovation at their core, is to ask at least a few dumb questions and make a few dumb comments every day. Usually this gets a good laugh, but I'm serious. Innovation, initiative, and creative work have a similar quality to the best music remixers and recycling programs. They can use everything that we feed them. When in search of ideas, when we try, for example, to solve a problem or start imagining the thread to a show's theme, there is an inevitable moment when someone will have a thought, an idea, a glimpse of something that he or she will hesitate to share.

An internal voice will say something like: *Don't say this; it's stupid. People will think that it's ridiculous; they will judge me and I will be put in a position of vulnerabilities. Who do I think I am?* When trust is present, that voice from the war on imagination recedes into the background. To make sure I keep that voice at bay, I signal as a leader that before we even start the session, they can expect me to express dumb ideas and make dumb comments, despite the resistance of my own internal voice to never offer something dumb. The result is that often even an idea that seems inferior triggers something unexpected, even magical, and leads to a project that's better.

When trust is fostered in your team members because you invest time and focus on developing the three stages of caring, safety, and trust, magical things can happen. By signaling your willingness to make mistakes and show your vulnerabilities by being in touch with your inner voice, you encourage others to do the same. This is particularly true for people in visible, formal positions of leadership or influence.

Prepare to Be Wrong

The two worst signals that you can send to your team when pushing innovation and creativity through is to take credit for other people's idea and to act as if others only make mistakes. These two behaviors alone can destroy your efforts to build trust.

Creating, inventing, and discovering something new about the world involves emotional work, work that exposes not only the polished you but the vulnerabilities inside you and in your organization. And some of the biggest rewards from being emotionally involved through your work are to be seen and appreciated. It's very hard to build brilliant ideas if you don't leave room for your mistakes and for the volatile nature of emotions.

To Foster Trust with Your Customers, Clients, and Audience, They Need to Understand Your Logic but also Feel Your Heart and the Texture of Your Emotions. This Is the Only Way They Can Feel What's Real or What's More Alive

If the process of caring first and securing safety is true and important for your team, it's also true for clients, customers, audiences, and anyone else your organization or business serves. Who are the people you are serving? For each group, how do you show care first? How do you secure safety? Do you foster and measure the trust between you?

I find it hard to trust a company that calls me a target and wants to segment me. Again, words matter. There's an immense potential for companies and initiatives that want to work on radically improving the experience of clients from a place of compassion and love, not from a place of cynicism. As more and more customers around the world are looking for their activities to be further integrated into the rest of their lives, the principle of experiences will continue to take space as an interface between commerce and customers. That trust is never stronger than when your clients feel your care and safety.

Make a Diamond out of Silos

Even if everyone complains about silos, they can become comfortable when you don't trust people around you, and it's easier not to trust people you don't know or know of but not directly. In a perverse way, silos can give a false impression of safety, of control over our fiefdom, our department, our team.

When I consider the most fundamental functions of most organizations, the operation, business, marketing and brand, production and creation-design, I see the potential for a diamond to form. The challenge is to harness the collective superpower stemming from the common work from those different parts of the same organization. We know that typically, this is not easy to do in small to large groups, with different interests.

When you scan your surroundings at work, is it possible that there is one person, one department, one group that works in a silo that you'd like to help change? Could identifying one sector, one function of your organization, and developing an initiative to know more about them, their preoccupations, and deeper aspirations help you discover things you didn't know about them? How much do you really know about that group that you might be complaining about or disapprove of, and how much do they really know about you and your team? If you have a group in mind, what could you do to start with caring first? How could you secure safety and then engage in fostering trust? Often we never speak to the groups in silos, perpetuating what we decry. Who on your team is most able to build bridges between people, ideas, teams? If it's you, what are you waiting for? If you don't have such a person in your team, how can this reflect on your next hire or your next training? I believe that the ability to build bridges between people of diverse backgrounds and divergent interests will be one of the most prized and searched for soft skills to go beyond the war on imagination. Learning to solve problems by sharing strengths rather than by sharing position through hierarchy can be a powerful way to connect the untapped potential of the diamond inside your organization.

Communicate Authentically

This is worth adding to our practice list. I predict that people's radar for cynicism will only expand over the coming years, so anyone who shows even a modicum of authenticity will be preferred in contrast. If the engagement of your employees is important to you, you must back it up in a way that's engaging. If you communicate with your team and your employees, don't pretend. Be real with them even if the news you are bringing is not great. You will always win respect in the long run.

People don't want a sales pitch. They want to know that you see them, understand their plights and the perils ahead, and even understand their fantasies.

Assess Your Fit with Your Organization

Fostering trust around you can also help you assess the threshold for collaboration in your organization. If you yearn to create more with a collective mind-set but hit too much resistance, you might be in a better position afterward to evaluate if the organization you are in is a good fit for you.

Exercises

The role of creative director at Cirque du Soleil is somewhat unique, although when I think of the responsibilities attached to the position, Don Draper, the creative director of the advertising agency Sterling Cooper on the TV show *Mad Men*, comes to mind. Traditionally there is a tension between the creative director and the production manager of a project. One leads the creative destiny and the other the realization of the project and the negotiation of the entire creative and technical team. In the spirit of fostering trust on MJ ONE, I spent a lot of time from the start working with my exceptional production manager, Michel Rioux, to care first and secure safety. Instead of considering him an adversary or just an enabler of the Creation team, I communicated to him my hope that we'd be partners. A lot of the success of the creation and production of MJ ONE stems from the fact that Michel and I decided to foster that trust despite the history of a tense and at times destructive relationship between these two important roles.

Do you have in your organization or through your work, positions, roles, or functions that by tradition and history have not developed a great relationship with people from your sector? What if you chose one person you work with to start caring first, finding out his or her aspirations and discovering at least one of that person's superpowers? What would a virtual net look like and what would it protect? Would it be about the information that you share or something else? What would you do to foster trust and increase collaboration if you were to build an emotional connection rather than simply a transactional one? What if that made all the difference in the world?

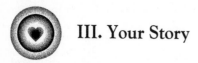 **III. Your Story**

Summary

Fostering trust is hard but rewarding work, as is collaboration. It requires us to let go of the remnant of our cynicism, a vestige of the war on imagination, so we can embrace more of our vulnerabilities and what makes us real and human. We all respond to what is real or what we perceive as real.

Fostering trust has four dimensions:

1. *Trust is the foundation of great collaboration and critical to superior innovation.* Separating the activity of collaboration from being in a collective, on a team, or in a group helps in understanding the importance of fostering trust. We can design our environment with collaborative work and trust in mind.

2. *We yearn for the universal.* Fostering trust in those around us often reveals that what we yearned for, others yearned for too.

3. *Expand trust in your role's potential.* Foster trust in your work, your role, and the fact that it's a platform for you to expand your ability to influence positively.

4. *Create with compassion and fierce originality for those you serve.* Foster trust in your clients, customers, and audiences, as often as you focus on internal growth, but do not use clients merely as instruments of that growth. Nobody wants to be a target or a demographic. If you ask most people what label they'd prefer if the only choice available was between *customer* and *human*, *human* would probably win. Therefore, you should ultimately create for humans and create in the name of life.

When you realize that the team that you are on doesn't always have great collaborative practices, naturally you are shocked and offended, and perhaps take it personally. You may think your team doesn't collaborate because they don't love you and don't appreciate who you are, and you are the victim. They don't get you, but you see further than they do, you think. But is that true? I discovered that once I thought that being on a team meant that we were meant to collaborate. Like that famous saying about love, I didn't realize until then that *collaborate* is actually a verb and is meant to be active.

Don't be fooled by teams, even by people all dressed the same and sharing the same logo and name. Being on a team doesn't mean being in a collaborative environment. I've been on projects at Cirque du Soleil that were deeply collaborative and others where we were a team but not truly collaborating to our full potential.

Act as if you only have influence but no authority so you can favor more dialogues, listening sessions, and activities where you genuinely learn from your constituents, leaders, employees, and colleagues. In other words, act as if you have no authority and an infinite amount of influence.

Remember Why This Matters

The combination of caring first (for ourselves and others), securing enough safety in our environment, and fostering trust together offers the courage to engage in one of the most serious and critical activities related to creativity, imagination, and innovation: playing with concepts, ideas, memories, things related and unrelated to each other.

Caring first is a foundational practice that we can continue to revisit and perfect as we and our organization continue to grow. Securing safety helps create demonstrable virtual and physical safety nets, proving the concrete importance that we give to physical and psychological safety for us and our teams. Finally, fostering trust helps nurture a collaborative mind-set in action. Beyond the psychological, cultural, and humanist benefits of fostering trust within your organization, these three interconnected stages create favorable conditions to start moving to the next stage. There are infinite numbers of approaches to playing, but one that is supremely relevant to improving our creative and innovative quotient points to playing with danger and limitations.

Checklist

- Consider the most fundamental functions and/or departments within your organization. What would happen if you developed the thinking about an upcoming project by going beyond the usual flow of decision making to integrate representatives from those different functions from the start? What would happen if you aligned more of the elements of your own organizational diamond?

- Collaboration is trust in action. Fostering trust means focusing on the quality of your current collaborations and improving them if needed. How would you qualify your current collaborations? Where do you feel that a boost of energy and a focus on caring first, securing safety, and fostering trust might benefit the most?

- Groups tend to work in silos unless collaboration becomes a working principle. Collaboration designed for your organization is possible and ideal.

- Fostering trust is about working more with your influence than with any authority. Do you rely more on your authority to get things done? Do you need to push through new, innovative work? How would you do your work if tomorrow you had no more authority but an infinite amount of influence to still do your work? You'd be the CEO, the director, the manager, the receptionist, the financial analyst but without a title, just with a carte blanche of influence. How would you foster trust around you?

- If your organization is well integrated from the inside, can you say the same on the outside with your customers, clients, and audiences? Are your customers and you in silos when it comes to innovation?

- Are there obvious things in your physical environment that promote trust and collaboration?

- What in your physical environment discourages trust and collaboration?

CHAPTER 5

Play with Danger

When the Stakes Are So High That We Just Want to Play It Safe

The future of innovation is no longer in the hands of the scientists, artists or designers working alone in a lab, loft or studio. . . . It is a creative, collective, humanist enterprise that seeks to find new solutions to the problems of our planet and its future.

Lucas Dietrich[1]

When caring, safety, and trust are established, we can focus on having constructive emotional responses to our experiences. This is also true for our audiences and the various other people we serve with our work. If we just play it safe with our offerings, we miss the opportunity to create that constructive emotional reaction that will make us memorable and relevant. By playing with danger and limitations, we can tap into the potential to make our work more resonant or important. By playing it safe because we feel that the stakes are too high, we risk our relevance over time. In other words, the stakes are too high to not play with danger and limitations.

I. Raising the Curtain

What's behind the joy and the enchantment that we can feel when we see someone jump higher and higher on a trampoline? And why is the source of that enchantment common to everything that we consider positive and memorable?

The Sage of the Acrobatic World

One of my favorite stories from my years at Cirque du Soleil comes from one of my favorite people there. Boris Verkhovsky is a sage of the acrobatic and performance world, an astute psychologist of the everyday life, and someone who truly understands the value of playing in the process of cultivating breakthroughs, something every manager should pay close attention to. When I left Cirque du Soleil in 2016, Boris was then director of the acrobatic and coaching team. A few years after I arrived at Cirque, he told me a story that still inspires me years later.

In the early 1980s, just before Cirque du Soleil was founded, lots of kids, including me, were dreaming of having a trampoline in the backyard. You already know that if I told my parents that, they would have asked me, *How many kids have already died this year from a fall on a trampoline? Do you want to be the next one?*

Trampoline History and Innovation

The origins of the trampoline are ancient. Forms of human air propulsion were present among the First Nations, the Inuit, in Canada, where a group of people used a dried animal skin to push in the air one person placed in the middle, making that person fly repeatedly. The trampoline has known many cycles of renewed popularity since its modern iteration before World War II. Few among us haven't dreamed of bouncing freely, carelessly, and heroically on the stretched fabric over a steel frame, jumping higher and higher in a rush of fun and fear. I wanted to dismantle in an instant any intention of well-orderedness elaborated by my parents and infuriating them when they eventually discovered my deed. A trampoline offered a chance to break free of that forbidden dream.

For circus arts, sports performance development, and even the training of astronauts, trampolines became part of the standard toolbox early in their existence. Georges Nissen, the credited inventor of the modern trampoline, kept innovating. In the 1960s, he introduced a new sport of his own design, Spaceball: a mix of basketball and volleyball on a trampoline, with goals recalling those of lacrosse or hockey. Since then, innovations using trampolines and movement have continued in many different directions.

Dedicated to creating something unexpected, Cirque, like Nissen, looked for ways to reimagine, reinvent, and innovate on how performances were presented and how they could enchant audiences.

A few years before I joined Cirque du Soleil, around 1992, during the creation of the show *Mystere* in Las Vegas, Boris and the creative team were looking for a place install a trampoline for artists' training during the creation of the show. A major nonstarter for experts in trampoline is that you can't, under any circumstances, put a trampoline next to a wall. Both from a standpoint of performance (bouncing height) and safety, they wanted to make sure that they could find a space in the theater training space for the trampoline to stand alone, away from any walls. The problem is that they couldn't find any such space and had to resign themselves to putting the trampoline in a corner, adding padding on the two walls and cautioning the artists to jump mindfully and with care. But sure enough, after a few days, other cast members would start to experiment, and a game emerged where the jumpers would integrate the wall during some of their training. None of these new tricks were integrated into the show, but Boris and his team noticed the reaction of passersby in the training studio when the artists would train and fool around. The emotional reaction, how startled they were, gave Boris the idea that maybe there was something there.

During the creation of the show *La Nouba* in 1996 (the show opened in 1998), the team at Cirque had the idea of formally combining wall and trampoline into one element of performance. Performers could now jump on the trampoline and then walk, midair, a few steps sideways on the wall, return to the trampoline, then walk on the wall and so on. In all my childhood dreams, I'd never imagined jumping from my parents' bed (while they were not looking) to walk on a wall next to the mattress! Although I'm not an acrobat, I've been privileged to see how their mind-set is being daredevils. Like skateboarders and other extreme sport explorers, acrobats work hard at mastering a move, a trick, a sequence, only to push the boundaries again once a move is done.

When it was time to integrate the first replacements for the original cast of *La Nouba*, Cirque invited some of the best trampoline athletes in the world to a workshop in Montreal to show them what was possible on this unique setup of trampoline-wall and offer eventual contract to the best of them.[2] Although the team was making progress on this new apparatus, none seem able to jump from the trampoline to the top edge of the wall. This movement was proving elusive, even downright scary, for even the most intrepid trampoline athletes among them. After a month, mounting doubts and frustration grew. Was it even possible without avoiding serious injuries? Had they invested all that time, effort, and resources for not much gain? Boris and one of his coaching partners had the idea of transforming the goal to achieve this seemingly impossible movement into a game.

Transforming the Goal into a Game

The next day, when the small team arrived at the studio in Montreal, they saw a bottle of liquor at the top of the wall that Boris had one of the technicians place there. He said that the first to reach the bottle would be able to take it home. Other than a growing familiarity with the difficulty of the challenge, nothing much had changed other than the context—suddenly, this was a game. For a moment at least, the athletes, the technical staff, the artistic coach, the director, and the producer were not under the spell of the mounting daily studio cost, of results to report on, of the pressure of failing or even winning. Now that it was just a game, the team could relax a bit.

On the next jump after this challenge was called, one of the top athletes in the group managed to jump on the top edge of the wall and bring back the bottle. A few days after the challenge was first announced, all of the team members had succeed in reaching the top edge of the small platform on the wall and were going beyond the original goal. What had seemed extraordinary started to become familiar, and fun, for all of them. As they changed their mind-set when faced with seemingly unsurmountable obstacles, playing became the linchpin of their breakthrough. This was literally a play with concrete danger, something that had previously seemed unreasonable to a small group of top performers.

When the audience saw the act for the first time in 1998, they could feel the discovery and the breakthrough even though they didn't know anything about the details of the development of the performance. Beyond the stunning visual act, the enchantment came from experiencing a constructive emotional reaction to something that not only felt original, authentic, and skillful, but the fruit of years of combined human efforts hidden in something beautiful to see.

Understanding the Need to Play

If we take the position of our customers, clients, and everybody else we serve through our work, we probably know that most of them, like us, are attracted to experiences, products, and services that trigger a constructive emotional response. There is a lot of emphasis today on the importance of story and storytelling to create that emotional response. And I'd argue that what most audiences or customers around the world yearn for primarily is to feel the story more than to know or understand every detail of what's told, at least if they must choose. I believe that this is true in narrative-heavy sectors like films, video games, and books. In part, we arrive at any experience with our own internal narrative, articulated or broken, conscious or not.

Even for the safest and most mundane products and services (think of your favorite soap, shampoo, or grocery store, for example), we still expect to experience a degree of positive emotional response from those encounters and transactions. We react to colors, the instructions provided, the packaging, the way people talked to us while serving and selling the product to us (e.g., if they smiled), even the font and graphic design on packages or online. Whatever the experience we have as audience or client, we want to relate, and when we do, we feel good, or inspired, or mobilized, or soothed, or puzzled.

As leaders of organizations, we should be driven to create experiences, products, or services that people will relate to emotionally and constructively. As simple as this might sound, my experience suggests how difficult it can be to design the conditions for that connection to happen and how much it matters to deepen our practice of leveraging the innovative process and its untapped potential.

Creating Emotional Electricity and Connection

Has anyone ever told you that the thing they liked best about a Broadway show they saw was that *the production really played it safe from the beginning to the end?* Can you imagine a show poster, a trailer for an Oscar-winning film, or a film director who says: *It's an exciting project where my team played it even safer than ever before! You will not be surprised, but everything is well managed, starting with your expectations. Come see it today!*

Even a fashion luxury platform like Modist chooses to soar and to stand out while selling restraint and humility. It proposes a "luxury modest style for extraordinary women" that originates from an intention of securing safety and fostering trust, but with daring beauty as the objective. The aim is to create a deep emotional connection with the promise of the brand—clothes you can feel beautiful in even if you adhere to a culturally different and personal definition of modesty: celebrating beauty through modesty, an out-of-the-box approach for Westerners who more often associate beauty with liberation, freedom, self-expression, and sensual overtness or affirmation.

So even when your core business can be perceived as deeply safe, the way to create an emotional connection is through daring—some form of emotional electricity that will resonate constructively with your audience or customers. This emotional connection is the reason that companies as diverse as Nike, Boeing, Emirates airline, Apple, the Yankees, and HSBC, to name a few, are prepared to spend significant resources to make sure that their audience not only *knows* about their story but *feels* it in their bones and their hearts.

Boris and his team could have played it safe, but it wasn't in the DNA of the company's founders or in him. A constructive emotional reaction doesn't need to exclusively be the source of happiness or good feelings. Being inspired by tough, challenging questions, called on by hard realities portrayed in a film, a book we read, or advertising, can also lead to constructive emotional reaction that eventually helps us to grow.

From the point of view of the performers, when you embark on a new creative project like that workshop was, your emotional connection to the project makes a difference too. Creating something new is hard, even painful. By definition, making something groundbreaking happen supposes meeting danger and limitations along the way. You can't be certain that you have the right resources, and the unknown creates worries, doubts, and uncertainty that is a primary source of danger.

When caring, safety, and trust have been established, a constructive emotional connection also happens within the members of the team. This connection builds the creative courage to go through the inevitable pain of groundbreaking work. Playing can facilitate that process if the groundwork was done before.

Playing with Danger and Limitation

Why can someone jumping on a trampoline enchant us at some times but not others? Experiences are relevant to us (we remember them or even recall them fondly) because they trigger a positive or constructive emotional response within us. To access that potential to feel the story that someone shares with us rather than simply see or hear that story, we need to be willing, as workers, creators, and leaders, to also play with danger and limitations. When we see someone playing with danger (perceived, metaphorical, or real) and eventually overcoming it, we are moved, inspired, and energized. We recognize intuitively in that moment our own victories and losses during a battle with danger and limitations.

For us, playing with danger and limitations means that we are willing to push the boundaries of our paradigms, our known confines, not only through rigor or rigid seriousness but playful questioning and scenarios. It's not that we eliminate rigor. Rather, we are adding to our toolbox the mindset of playfulness as a way to tackle some of our most challenging problems. It also means becoming mentally agile at using the inevitable obstacles and other limitations to what we are trying to create playfully, integrating them into the design of our work.

We systematically transform every limitation through playfulness. We learn to see every limitation as a riddle to solve instead of a personal attack or something that can only leave us a victim. To do that, we get inspired by the things we love and the games we play, and we adapt them to make our teams move together, have fun, and set them up for success.

There is no unique formula or recipe; everybody has different ways to play and be playful. The process of integrating play within our innovation process and, more broadly, within our work culture is also a chance to practice playfulness through our imagination and creativity. It's a practice where everyone can benefit, a chance for our superpowers to shine, and we can discover the superpowers in the people around us.

It's normal to play it safe, and it can be the best decision to take in the face of difficult challenges. Wanting to innovate on all fronts at the same time can put any organization at risk. When the war on imagination is waged inside a company, however, the risk is that playing it safe becomes the default position, no matter the company's innovating past. Many companies that at some point were the unassailable champion of their category or industry nevertheless fell, quickly or slowly, into irrelevance.

When playing it safe becomes our only play, either because we think that the stakes are too high or the situation is dire, we expose ourselves and our business to fatal insignificance and, by extension, becoming unmemorable. We usually start to play it safe when we think only of the important bottom line but not of what I call the *high line*—the company's engagement with its own superpowers and genius. We might even hear from our colleagues exactly that: here they will play it safe because no one wants to create trouble for this project.

We saw that playing with danger and limitation also develops your creative courage, the mental fortitude to see obstacles with a sense of play, with a call to challenge the status quo. No matter the budget, resources, and time available, every project, creative or not, will face limitations at some point. Moreover, when you dream of breaking through by creating something that will inspire, surprise, or persuade your customers to change, transform, or engage, the chances that you will need to take a risk are high.

As our world gets more connected and our technologies become even more powerful and pervasive, the threshold to inspire, surprise, and persuade shifts, becoming less stable, predictable, and containable.

Eccentric Collaboration

Boris showed care first to the team of newcomers, secured enough safety and trust for the team to be willing to take risks by playing with danger and the limitations that they faced in time, resources, and venturing into new territory. The innovation in their approach also included another element of play that I call *eccentric collaboration*. In this case, the collaborations were physical, between the wall and the trampoline, and relational, between experts from the circus who had a background in sports acrobatics and trampoline athletes who knew nothing or just a bit about the world of entertainment but specialized in their sport's discipline. The result was a resounding success that not only inspired a generation of athletes and artists, but started an entire industry of trampo-wall parks across the world.

How to Overcome Playing It Safe by Default

It's possible to infuse anything that we create with a virtual door to this constructive emotional connection between our customers, audiences, and clients and the products, services, and experiences that we create for them. It's possible to do the same thing inside our organization with our teams, colleagues, and communities. To do that requires being prepared to play with danger and limitations. This allows us to discover unexpected new spaces of possibilities and abilities, and this transforms our attitude when we inevitably face obstacles. We open the door to bring energy and vibrancy into our work.

This is not about nurturing a blindly positive mind-set. As we stop being a victim of the war on imagination by caring first, securing safety, and fostering enough trust to be ready to move past fears, doubts, and limitations, we develop the physical and mental fortitude to play in the most difficult moments. That fortitude also helps us tap into another superpower that we can all develop: intuition.

For our most critical challenges, finding solutions through play often involves a community. When we face immense challenges, especially when we are in formal leadership positions and roles, we can tend to go it alone or consult others only at the last minute, letting everyone become slightly miffed at trying to accomplish a lot in little time. Giving space and time for people around you to surprise you with their ideas and to make mistakes is critical to make play work.

If play is not part of the culture at work, start small. There are many ways to integrate and adapt already explored and well-established ideas, from old-fashioned contests that can involve an entire community at work to models creating communities of interests and one-on-one exchanges of ideas and skills like what E-180 does with its Braindates.[3] Hackathon- and Museomix-style events can also open the gates to play.[4] There are many genuine ways to include your community through events that open the process of innovation to a greater group rather than a select few at the top of your organization.[5] These events have the added benefits of helping players identify future talents, unknown because of the role they currently play within your group.

 ## II. Insights

Practices

Not every organization is ready to integrate play within its process, but every organization can use playing with danger and limitations once it feels that the work on caring, safety, and trust is established. Otherwise, to integrate play without caring first will feel manipulative. If we introduce it without securing enough safety, it risks feeling trivial. And activating play without trust will invoke something fake. The stronger our foundation is, the further away is the cynicism of the war on imagination and the readier we are to use playing with danger and limitations as an important stepping-stone in our work toward deeper innovation.

Most often, danger in our case will be a metaphor or it will be virtual, although leading or trying to transform the world around us always comes with risks that can at times translate into concrete, physical danger. Integrating play in your life allows you to translate your positive experience at work.

Strive for Eccentric Collaborations

We develop routines and ways of working that ensure as much efficiency as possible and help us cope with and thrive on the world's complexity. We have our favored collaborators, partners, and colleagues, and the nature of our work sets practices that are useful and vital to the flow of our work. Yet this situation can also prevent us from taking advantage of the potential collaborations inside our organization (with other departments and other colleagues) and outside our organization (with, e.g., other vendors, businesses, cities).

Of course, there's nothing new to collaborations and partnerships inside and outside organizations and businesses. What I advocate for in the spirit of playing with danger and limitations is eccentric collaborations around projects that will stretch the imagination of both entities to produce something truly unexpected. The project might be participating in the needed reinvention of a sector of your organization or the projection of that sector into the future. By nature, eccentric collaborations almost inevitably lead to creating and playing.

No one expected the collaboration I creatively spearheaded between Cirque du Soleil and Verity Studio, founded by prolific scientist, inventor, creator, and entrepreneur Raffaello D'Andrea. How could we bridge the ultimate gap between the warmth of human emotions in performance and the implacable precision of the drones that Verity believes "will fundamentally transform the live event experience"?[6] We ended up creating together a short film called *Sparked*, the fruit of the creative input of both entities, and we learned a lot about the eventual implementation of drones in a live performance.

As clients, customers, and citizens, we might also see how the opportunities to instigate eccentric collaborations abound in different sectors. Ultimately, what these eccentric collaborations can allow us to do is create projects that are easier to contain and help us peek into a potential future. They feed our efforts toward innovation and leverage the mind-set of playing with limitation and danger. There's an incredible power in mixing things that don't seem to fit together at first or to find common ground between elements that might be considered at the extremes. Even if the result of the collaboration is not concrete enough, the participating entities and their people learn tremendously from the initiatives.

One of the determining factors in the foundation of Cirque du Soleil's success is that it was not dogmatic in inviting artists and athletes alike to work together in a multidisciplinary way. For most circuses, even those coming from the new circus movement at the end of the 1970s and early 1980s, there was something almost blasphemous in mixing circus artists with anyone else. Circus artists worked on their side, artists from the performing arts like dancers and musicians worked on their side, and athletes like gymnasts on yet another side. In the same spirit, people from the work of theater would not usually mix with those of the circus.

Cirque had the creative courage to bring everyone together under one tent to create something that felt fresh, unusual, and relevant. Today, it's less countercultural than it was in the past to function that way, but it was a form of eccentric collaboration at the time that had a global impact on live entertainment. These nondogmatic connections fly straight in the face of the war on imagination, and they open new territories of innovation to those willing to see through the invisible.

Make It Punk Rock!

When I worked with Jamie Kin to create MJ ONE in Las Vegas, he came up with an expression that reflected his will to create the show without being trapped by tradition or convention.[7] He wanted to inspire the team to be mindful of the reasons for our creative choices. Were we making choices because that's the way things usually were done at Cirque du Soleil, or because this was going to serve the experience that we were trying to create?

I adopted the expression, and made it mine, that what we were doing was punk rock, badass in spirit. While MJ ONE has nothing directly connected to a punk rock show, the idea here is that in a spirit of playfulness and transforming danger and limitations into advantage, every project and initiative where innovation drives can benefit from an infusion of punk rock spirit into it. It's something that makes the project not overtly respectful of the status quo and of the danger and the limitations it faces. Adding a spirit of punk rock to your project invites you to prevent becoming obsequious to your traditions and paradigm, therefore making you that much readier to play with limitations and danger.

Play, Don't Think

Playing with danger and limitations invites us to think less and do more while having fun. Far from discouraging thinking, thinking alone is often not enough to tackle our biggest challenges. The advice of most sports experts is that great players don't think when they play.

Create a Safe Place to Play Dangerously

Innovation labs and innovation initiatives usually happen at this stage of playing with danger. At Cirque du Soleil, I had the opportunity to launch a long-standing initiative through a lab dedicated to innovation. Over the years, Cirque had launched projects that didn't work as well as expected. The most successful research was happening in part during the process of workshops, before the creation started, but these were costly, their outcome was uncertain, and even if they seemed successful, their use in a show was itself haphazard.

The other successful source of innovation was the creation of the shows themselves. Through the hotbed of creating a show over eighteen to thirty-six months, opportunities, challenges, and problems emerged, and some solutions led to breakthroughs. C-Lab was a new initiative, imagined by the marketing team and adopted and developed by our creative department. This was a chance to have a dedicated space outside our costume and set workshops where we could build imperfect things with our hands, meet creative collaborators, and organize the creative work.

In preparation for the internal launch of the innovation lab, we wanted to have a physical and visible space that would become its storefront. I pushed for something daring in the space, and we ended up with one-third of the space designed with a foam pit that evoked our origin and could be used for small creative sessions or meetings. You'd remove your shoes and jump into the foam pit with your guess. What's interesting is that every time there was a public relations event, media wanted to interview us in that foam pit, but from a practical standpoint, few meetings were held there. Why did it fail from that standpoint? Why did this space that was so playful not work?

For the mind-set of play to work, you need to have a solid foundation. Anchoring caring, safety, and trust is fundamental to creating the proper environment for play to be effective. Although the collective tradition of the company was filled with the idea of playing with challenges, this is never something that you can take for granted in any organization. In a context of profound transformation and seeing people seemingly relaxing, having a creative session in a foam pit was uncomfortable for some of our leaders.

The war on imagination often emerges through profound transformation, when a company is in the process of writing a new chapter. People coming into the lab space didn't feel safe enough to plunge into the foam pit themselves. There was not enough trust to relax and play. It's important to recognize the right moment for play to happen, and a good indicator is that trust is growing; it's present and intentionally fostered. The principle is simple: the more dangerous and ambitious you want to be in exploring and innovating, the safer and more trustworthy the environment must be.

Boost Empathy for the Process of Innovation

Risks are connected with the creation of any lab dedicated to innovation in an organization. If this process is wrongly communicated or designed, it can send the wrong message that innovation, creativity, and imagination are contained inside a box on floor XYZ of your organization.

Whenever you can, even with a dedicated team, make the whole organization open to creativity, imagination, and innovation. Ensure clear bridges, doors, and access for people who are outside the daily life of innovation but would like to contribute. Ensure as well that everyone is well versed on your current process of innovation and the aspirations you and your teams have. Finally, and critically, encourage your business teams, operations teams, and production teams to not only know about the creative process but to live that process at the forefront.

The lack of empathy caused by a simple lack of understanding of the process of ideation, discovery, and innovation can cost companies dearly in ill-designed plans that didn't correctly integrate the innovation process. Make sure that anyone outside the direct process understands it. Creativity and innovation can be celebrated without creating an elite group that disconnects from its larger community and vice versa.

Hanna Rossin wrote a much-discussed article about what she called "the overprotected kid": the obsession of parents for the safety of their kids risked developing adults averse to risk taking, messiness, and confronting danger. That concern could also be applied to adults. Playing with danger and limitations invites us to welcome and leverage messiness for the benefit of all of us. If we try to control everything, the only thing we risk discovering is that we can't do that.[8]

Remember the Increment and Sequential Stages

Although we can look at every stage individually and focus our work or attention on the one that seems the most pressing, I can't insist enough on the incremental and sequential nature of these stages. It's worth repeating that each of them is as strong as the ones preceding it and that our mastery of them can continue to deepen no matter where we are as an organization in our development and no matter what type of organization we are. Fostering trust sets a path to play with danger and limitation. Playing with danger and limitations reinforces trust if trust was there in the first place.

Exercises

Everything that needs practice and can be practiced is a bridge to create a game and play. Try these exercises:

- When is the last time that you played with your colleagues? What was the experience like? What would you do the same again if you could? What would you change?

- What do you play at? What are your favorite games, sports, and activities, inside and outside? Can you extend the experience to your colleagues? To further trust, play in a more relaxed setting first. This can be a way to learn to play with your closest collaborators. During the creation of *MJ ONE* in Las Vegas, we decided to celebrate the theme of the city and created a ritual of playing poker almost every Saturday with the core team. Although we didn't talk much about the work, our work benefited immensely from those simple moments of fun together.

- What are you the most afraid of for your project, company, or business?

- What are the biggest limitations that you face?

- What are the biggest limitations that your project, company, or business faces?

- What superpowers do you have that can't necessarily transform limitations? Who collectively has those superpowers in your organization?

- What are the biggest paradigms in your organizations?

- What are your biggest objectives this year? What would be symbolic of the bottle, the wall, and the trampoline if you were to play at inventing a new way to achieve these objectives?

- What's in need of reinvention at work? In your life?

- Think about five of the most fanciful, outrageous, and inspiring eccentric collaborations you could initiate with your organization. Go wild and don't worry about the feasibility yet. What would it take to make one happen? What would be your priority, and why?

- When I auditioned performers with my colleagues from Cirque du Soleil and elsewhere, we'd do icebreakers at the beginning of the session for everyone to connect to their sense of wonder, flow, and playfulness. Do you have a ritual or practices to break the ice playfully with your team? One of my favorites is to open with a morning reflection: five minutes when everyone produces something. It could be writing, a drawing, a graph, a chart. Then take another two minutes to share the highlights with the group.

- When's the last time that you played with your food? I mentioned in Chapter 2 that learning to cook together with your close team can be a transformative experience. Although I placed it in the practices of caring first, this can also be transformative in the context of playing with danger and limitation. You can easily create obstacles and contexts that your team can learn from while having fun.

- At Cirque, we sometimes moved together thanks to unique space in the studio dedicated to circus and aerial performances. There was a workshop where everyone would try different apparatus, like the flying ring, the German wheel, and the basic trampoline. The simple experience of moving together created immense pleasure and fostered trust among us. Can you find ways to move with your team regularly?

- Is there someone passionate about games on your team who could contribute to your reflection?

- Look into the past of the inventors and pioneers of your industry or sector of activity for clues. From past or failed innovations, you could discover initiatives that had been abandoned but now could be uplifted, upgraded, and revitalized. Many ideas have been produced but fell into oblivion or didn't work that well at the time.

- Sketching your ideas and concepts is a valuable way to explore individual play with danger and limitations.

- Collective painting, learning a sport together, and many other practices can help build genuine memories.

- Play with symbols. During the creation of MJ ONE, after every jam with the producers, I met with the creative team the next morning to share the notes and comments from the executive team. I would often wear a T-shirt with the picture of a fox to remind everyone that we were astute and that even if sometimes the process was difficult and we were tired, we were as smart as foxes. Depending on your situation and context, you have infinite possibilities for assigning symbols to what you wear and send overt or subtle positive messages to yourself or your team. Play with symbols.

- Design this game for your challenges. It's much more fun and unpredictable if you play with at least two other people and mix your responses at the end.

  1. Identify an area of your work or your organization that needs reinvention.

  2. Complete this written statement: Reinventing _____ to _____ our employees/clients/customers/etc. Example: Reinvent the trampoline to enchant our audience.

  3. Introduce something unexpected that could help the reinvention process. List many options, if possible, before choosing one.

  4. Merge what needs reinvention with a new element, creating something new. It's not important at this point if that mental construction exists in the real world. Ideally, they've never before or not recently been merged into one. This introduction of a new element, object, or concept should help elevate the situation, like the wall did for the trampoline.

  5. Add an obstacle related to your industry—something related to why there's a need for reinvention.

  6. Add a motivation—an incentive that's playful that can help get rid of the obstacle.

  7. Bridge the gap. Answer this question: How can the new element and the initial situation (status quo) bring about the reinvention that I seek?

  8. Explore any discoveries, and reflect with your team or partner(s).

 ## III. Your Story

Summary

- Playing with danger and limitations is a fun path to discover breakthroughs.
- Everybody wants to have a constructive emotional reaction to what they experience, from buying toothpaste to choosing a new house.

This was also true at Cirque when I would sit with my colleagues to watch one of the shows in creation. In a live show, our emotional responses allow us to relate to what we see onstage and around us, and therefore to care for what's presented to us, evaluating if it makes sense for us. The importance of cultivating the emotional potential of an audience goes beyond focusing only on the spectacular. Even the most powerful technology can't compel as much as what constructive emotional experiences can do when smartly elicited.

- If they must choose between knowing a story and feeling one, most people choose to feel.

- I predict that playing and games will have an important role in the future evolution of business. When play can count on a solid foundation of stages like caring, safety, and trust in the background, it becomes legitimate and potentially powerful to support innovation initiatives.

- When the war on imagination reduces our vision, we focus only on the bottom line. We forget the high line or think that it's not important, and playing safe creeps into everything that we do.

When we play with danger and limitations, our creative courage grows. Playing also stimulates our universal ability to dream. I suspect that every great champion and artist enters a phase of dreaming, even if for a few seconds, before a breakthrough. I suspect that the same thing happened to the trampoline athletes in Montreal in 1996. They saw the bottle of liquor, started to relax, remembered how they had once jumped on their parents' bed and how free they felt then. As they relaxed into play, they forgot to think so much and started to dream.

Creators from various disciplines and backgrounds have suggested that everything we create, we make twice—first in our head, through plans, visualizations, drawings, and discussions, and then through realizing our vision in the physical world. In that spirit, I'd say that we start to innovate when we are willing to play with our limitations and the danger of working with uncertain outcomes and find ourselves dreaming effortlessly before a breakthrough emerges. It's a call to live like tight-wire artists, dancing at times on a low line, just a few feet from the ground, and then soaring to great heights, wire still tight, still dancing, with creative courage in their hearts. They show us how to dance on the bottom line, but they also invite us to live on the high line of vision. It doesn't matter how hard we try, we won't find in an Excel spreadsheet what moves our teams, employees, audiences, clients, and customers. It's not that spreadsheets don't matter; they are just not what the ultimate focus should be. The minute your ultimate focus is on the spreadsheet, you are close to dead. What moves people and mobilizes them is always composed of dreams.

Checklist

- When there is a real innovation process with play, power is at bay. In any organization, the lab or creative center is also a place of power. In other words, creativity and innovation attract everyone inside the organization because most people want to express something. If your organization does a great job at identifying people's aspirations, superpowers, and genius and puts approaches and support in place for those to be honed and shared, there are no issues with your process becoming a free-for-all.

- The more we close that process to others, the less this process can renew itself. One way to avoid suffocating your process of innovation is to ensure the circulation of people and ideas around your core team. One concrete way to connect your innovation center and process to its potential is to invite younger generations, even those still in high school, and older generations to work side by side around projects. Those young ones will revolutionize the world tomorrow. When you have a couple of talented fifteen- and sixteen-year-olds hanging around your serious business, you know that you have an open process and not a free-for-all.

- Have a robust way to communicate with the outside world so you can gather and answer the questions from your community. Discover from them new missions and refine your message on what you are looking for and what is not useful.

CHAPTER 6

Dream

Spreadsheets Don't Dream Yet

I hear a faint voice deep inside me singing joyfully: "See. It can be done!"
Philippe Petit[1]

I. Raising the Curtain

On August 6, 1974, Philippe Petit, the acclaimed French multidisciplinary artist and high-wire poet, rose above the bottom line of our lives and made his way up to the empty space between the two towers of the World Trade Center, making the sky his impermanent stage. Startling New York City and the rest of the world, Petit walked, danced, and lay down on a wire, looking at the sky, in a state of grace, for about forty-five minutes. Everyone who noticed watched spellbound. His only safety was his balancing pole. His feat, which he called *the coup* and *the perfect crime*, has inspired films, books, and, I'm sure, countless artists and creators.[2]

Quintessentially not playing it safe, Philippe Petit, who had dreamed of accomplishing this since he was fourteen years old, created a performance at the intersection of an art installation, a provocative public stunt, and poetry in movement. He put his life at great risk, but he wasn't sponsored, and he wasn't paid. Instagram and the other social media platforms didn't even exist then. So why did he do it? When asked by a journalist, shortly after his arrest, he famously said: "The beauty of it is, there is no 'why.'" The energy from his work still resonates today.

Another Frenchmen I admire, the painter Henri Matisse, suggested that our most creative moments are found in the in-between instants of our lives when we are immersed in the unknown and forced to choose a direction forward. When we play with danger and limitations, we create opportunities to open a space of transition that eventually leads to breakthroughs. That intermediary space, that bridge, is always made of dreams. Some are pleasant and others daunting, but their composition is always that of dreams. Playing with danger, limitations, and breakthroughs opens the realm of dreams to infinite possibilities.

Cirque's Early Dreaming

Before Cirque du Soleil opened its first and second shows in Las Vegas, successively in 1993 and 1998, few people would have imagined the company benefiting from stratospheric success and recognition. First, Las Vegas was about gambling and a different kind of entertainment.

How could a circus without animals thrive in a land where Siegfried and Roy, the German-American duo of magicians who included lions and tigers in their routine, reigned supreme?

During the twentieth anniversary of Cirque du Soleil, a few of my colleagues and I saw a document from the late 1980s—a giant paper pad. It was neatly covered with objectives for the following five years, hand-written with markers of different colors. I learned that it was the result of a group brainstorm held by the executive team of the time, including Cirque's founder, Guy Laliberté. The group set out the most ambitious objectives they could articulate for the next five years of the company. It was meant to be as aspirational and bold as possible. There's no doubt that with a visionary entrepreneur like Guy in the room and such a talented group of pioneers, everyone pushed and was inspired to think as passionately as possible.

I don't remember the details of the document. What was remarkable was what was not there. I had the impression that I was a time traveler, able to consider the past through this pad, a testament to vision but my direct knowledge of what happened in the future. What stunned me was how ambitious those dreams were then—and they no longer seemed that ambitious to us. Not only had we surpassed all of them collectively, but it was even hard to imagine that those visionaries thought of these objectives as wildly ambitious.

An old saying is that we should be careful about what we wish for because we might just get it. Expanding on this idea, what's the point of banking on innovation as a powerful source to sustain or create new value if our objectives are purely defensive and only safe? A principle of creation is that even when we dream our wildest, boldest dreams, reality tends to overwhelm what we have conceived, showing more textures, nuances, and dimensions than we could have anticipated. Links emerged that we never would have attached to our dreams. So why play safe when dreaming? Why have safe dreams when the process of innovation and creativity suggests that even when we dream our most daring dreams, chances are that we will continue to open unexpected spaces for exploration and breakthroughs.

The Bottom Line, the Blade, and the Noose

When the war on imagination confines us to the bottom line, counting without dreaming of anything other than the earnings, the bottom line becomes a blade or a noose. When we try nonetheless to venture into innovation and creativity, we become intensely transactional. We forget to play, we forget to foster trust, we don't have time to care because we need to earn. We cut corners with our line transformed into a blade, or we catch the first rabbit in front of us with our noose. We don't know when to be patient and when to be impatient. We want each dollar we put in to generate at least the same amount. Ideally, our idea of wild success for our innovation is that our exploration must generate its own revenue and then some.

Magic happens without having to cultivate it. This is *magical thinking*—wanting everything without offering much. It's purely transactional and believes that generosity for its own sake is foolish and an insult to the return on investment. This is the sort of vision that the war on imagination encourages. When we try to innovate that way, we play it safe by wanting everything. We can still accomplish things, but we fall short of our potential, and progressively we fall.

The Wings and Magic of Dreams

Both Philippe Petit's dream when he was fourteen and Cirque du Soleil's bold early visions that led to decades of incomparable influence on popular culture and live entertainment have an aspirational quality that I call *impossible-beautiful*. This is the subjective, aspirational quality that we can confer on an objective, a vision, or a project to elevate its scope, ambition, and constructive influence. Impossible-beautiful is so beautiful that it feels impossible and so impossible that it's beautiful. It claims a sort of real magic in opposition to magical thinking. The power of the concept of impossible-beautiful is drawn directly from the space of dreams. Normal, conventional limitations and danger that we face in the physical world are contoured, distorted, remixed, and overcome with solutions. When we decide to claim our courage and reach even higher to a few of our projects, objectives, or vision, we confer real magic on our aspirations and collective potential. We create space for everyone to start dreaming about breakthroughs that we want yet seem impossible still.

We have access to that magic mostly through discovering how good we are at playing with danger and limitations. The poetry, potential, and power of giving at least a few of our projects an impossible-beautiful quality is not megalomania, grandiosity, blind positive thinking, or recklessness. It is not about subjecting others to our will or about thinking our way through any situation. It is certainly not about doing things without rigor. Imagining projects through the lens of the impossible-beautiful still demands the right amount of preparation so we can improvise. Impossible-beautiful can't happen if we don't care first for our team, or it will draw considerable recrimination and bitterness once the exploit is done. The impossible-beautiful filter encourages the consideration of others in our vision.

Invoking the impossible-beautiful in our personal work, the groove of the impossible-beautiful mind-set involves making the decision to welcome more beauty in our lives, to welcome the fact that inside all of us is an open space for genius to evolve and thrive. It's a space for mastery, virtuosity, and artistry that suggests practice, the right amount of patience, and learning through failing and then winning.

The mind-set and filter of the impossible-beautiful invokes the need for us as individuals to recognize that we are born to be instigators of that magic. That magic is in fact nothing more than the belief that if we are more generous and ambitious with the scope, breadth, and influence of our vision, we make our innovation initiative more relevant and more important. We are here to conceive of ways to discover the real magic of the impossible-beautiful filter—inexhaustible ways to nourish our lives. It starts with making a conscious decision to add the real magic of the impossible-beautiful mind-set to our vision and projects, which creates a bridge for a concrete manifestation of that thinking to happen in our real world. This commitment allows us to recognize the everyday magic around us because we become open to understanding and recognizing the implication of that real magic.

Legend has it that Newton discovered the laws of gravity while he was reflecting on the forces that animate nature and saw an apple fall from a tree. What if Newton wasn't practiced at discovering the impossible-beautiful laws of nature? How many people before him saw an apple fall from a tree without making the connections that he did? When you are prepared to set impossible-beautiful dreams, you ready yourself to recognize their attributes when they emerge like challenges to connect and solve.

Thinking Beautiful, Not Big

Playing releases space to dream. Real dreams by definition have an impossible-beautiful dimension and quality to them that gives depth to our collective aspirations and teeth to our innovation initiatives. It differs from clichés that we only need to think it to manifest it. Instead of thinking big to create value, we think beautiful.

As we face rapid transformation of our work, even uncertainty shifts in unpredictable ways. Today we are confronted regularly with the question of the significance of our individual and collective work. We can anticipate that question to become even more persistent in the future. What's the determining factor that makes our offerings resonate with our employees, team, audiences, customers, and clients?

When we think that we don't have time to dream because we don't have time to play, we default to thinking that the only way to create value is by becoming bigger or simply by offering something new. This is a trap that the war on imagination tends for its self-preservation.

Creating projects and visions through the impossible-beautiful filter and mind-set is not about bigger and new for its own sake, although these elements can be attributes of what you are trying to create. Novelty and size inflation alone rarely make a convincing case for mass appeal and resonance. Making your project impossible-beautiful calls on us to outdo ourselves by bringing more relevant beauty into the world. What's useful is beautiful; what inspires is beautiful; what offers solutions to our greatest challenges and issues is beautiful. The world has infinite space for beauty and love, which are infinitely renewable resources.

As critically important as spreadsheets and earnings are, you can't extract impossible beauty out of them. But the people you serve inside and outside your organization long for more impossible beauty. In part, that's what made Cirque du Soleil so resonant and successful. It drew an impossible beauty that came from its hunger to discover the world and from the passion it communicated. People are moved by beauty and by the impossible happening in front of their eyes, not by spreadsheets.

 ## II. Insights

Practices

Value Emotional Work

As robots play increasingly crucial roles in our lives, more elements of what we do at work become commoditized.[3] One of the anticipated effects of this transformation, in my opinion, will be a premium on human connection, emotions, and interactions. As we live more through our screens and connected devices, the need to compensate at times with mediated or visceral human and life connections will rise. The value of constructive emotional responses and experiences will also become part of the activities and life passages that we experience. It is possible that we will shift from an era of brand relevance to one of constructive emotional relevance, but it's too early to tell.[4] As machines and smarter robots replace our work at a speed that we probably underestimate, the portion of our work that will be the most difficult to replace might be the smart emotional parts of what we do. Proportionally these parts might also gain the most value.

Moving People's Hearts

I would argue that we are all now in the business of moving people, of moving them emotionally, of touching their hearts genuinely, inside and outside our organizations. Our capacity to do this has a tremendous influence on our ability to innovate and create more relevant value for those we serve: banks, architectural firms, governments, airport mainte-nance companies, and cafés, for example. Without gaining access to the parts of your work that contain the potential for impossibly beautiful dreams, you risk offering an experience to your employees, teammates, and the people you serve that doesn't resonate emotionally as much as it could or, worse, lacks a potent dream.

Use Intuition

We don't give enough space to our intuition. In a world made more insightful and data smart, there is still space to express our creative leadership with analysis paired with intuition, at times with intuition driving some of our decisions. This is one of the only ways for us to access the space between logic and pure flight of fancy.

Be Ready for the Dreams

Paul Auster and Elizabeth Gilbert both refer to the importance of being ready when opportunities, ideas, and inspiration strike.[5] Dreaming of having Willie May's autograph, Auster tells his story of coming face to face with his baseball idol when he's eight years old. This is his chance to get the autograph, but he doesn't have a pen, and no one around him does either. From that moment on, Auster decides to always carry a pen on him.

Gilbert describes with words made almost physical how poet Ruth Stone would run from the plains where she worked as a child on her family farm all the way home when she heard a poem making its way to her from the hills. She would run and hurry home to capture as much as possible from the fleeting poem hissing and swooshing like the wind.

In both stories, being ready to catch fleeting ideas and glimpse your impossible-beautiful vision is important. And the more you take your ideas seriously, the stronger they tend to get because you also build trust within yourself and create space for dreams to emerge.

Be Generous with Space to Support Creativity and Innovation

We can dream and innovate anywhere. I don't believe that creative space design should be dedicated only to "creative types" in organizations. Rather it should influence every work space, from finance and information technology all the way to reception and the cafeteria.

Creatively Rearrange

Dreams love rearrangement because it allows them to bounce differently in the space. Rearrange from time to time. Choose movable as opposed to fixed furniture, which suggests rigidity. What I find supremely important for capturing and developing dreams is to create space that is as flexible as possible. This is particularly true for collective creative contexts. There is still much to explore and understand when it comes to creating space truly conducive to dreaming and great ideation. Consider these aspects of space:

- *Formal and informal play.* Creating flexible space offers an area for creative rearrangement and having set places to play formally (e.g., table tennis) and informally (abstract games like those created by Ludus Ludi that offer the possibility to think and play, alone or with others, inspire the eye, and unleash curiosity).[6]

- *Collective and solitary options.* There should be a mix of open space where people can meet and work in small teams but also places for quiet, focused, solitary time. Open plan spaces where no one can hide are not the best way to let dreams grow, although dreaming and innovation can happen in less-than-optimal spaces.

- *Walls.* Lots of fixed and, ideally, mobile walls that you can move with your hands, that you can roll around and that can change location over time. Ideation walls, small and big, are useful for physical, kinesthetic ideation and for displaying ideas. Rolling paper walls are a substitute for fixed walls and can double their function to offer isolation for more focused work in open-plan offices. Virtual ideation walls and clouds of visual inspirations are obviously good too, but I advocate, whenever it's possible, for a mix of digital/ virtual tools and physical/paper ones. Not out of nostalgia but because the variety of ways you capture ideas, from the context in which you are to the posture you adopt (standing, sitting, lying on the floor, etc.) affects your output, literally promotes seeing things from different perspectives.

Think and Dream in Movement

Moreover, different movements activate different points of view on the world and different ideas emerge. I suspect that if golf is popular among the business community for meetings, it is also for this added benefit of thinking in movement. Don't stay in the office. When you can, go for a walk and discuss ideas and challenges with your colleagues that way. Try doing it in unusual contexts too and see what happens—maybe on a chairlift or during a rock-climbing session. Move and practice dreaming.

Celebrate Mess

Having a messy room where almost anything goes is truly valuable. Think about carton paper put together with duct tape and tools to build ideas with our hands, not only our brains.

Don't Overlook Snacks and Rituals

A friend at the design firm IDEO inspired me when I visited its office in San Francisco. IDEO has a simple ritual at three o'clock every Wednesday: tea and cookies in the kitchen. No one is required to show up, but I suspect that not many people can resist the cookies and the incredible view of the Pacific Ocean.

You don't need to create a complex ritual, and a little bit of food always contributes to bringing people together. The bonfire was our first ancestral gathering place, and what our forebears felt back then is still inside us. Take advantage of that feeling to create your own version of the bonfire. In fact, that place of respite after hunting and gathering all day and hustling to survive must have been the first time that our ancestors started to dream while awake, processing their day, replaying the film of their triumphs and failures, troubleshooting, and dreaming.

Supporting the formation of dreams inside your organization simply means offering and reigniting simple rituals that you might have. This is very positive and in the spirit of creating informal connections that are unplanned and conducive to fostering new dreams.

Care for Your Dreams

When the war on imagination rages, dreams are laughed at or simply cajoled into submission. When the war is inside us, we don't need anyone to do the rejection, we become experts of "NO". Like ideas, dreams are sensitive, and although they have a sense of humor, they take it personally when we laugh at them and often hide for a while until they feel safe to return. Take your dreams seriously and offer to your organization that same commitment and passion about dream sacredness. The more we take those dreams and their articulation seriously, the more they surprise us.

Dreams have cousins. Coincidence is one of them. The more you get attuned, benevolent, attentive, and compassionate toward your dreams, the more agile you are at taking advantage of coincidences that tend to show up everywhere, sometimes challenging the laws of probability.

Mind mapping is a powerful and simple approach to gathering ideas. And in the process of articulating dreams, this is a tool worth trying to capture, catch, and generate ideas and bits of ideas without trying to group them or organize them right away. It was developed in its modern form in the 1950s and was popularized in the 1970s by Tony Buzan, who developed many tools dedicated to cognitive practices, and in the early 2000s by David Allen.[7]

An abundance of resources is available online for tools and methods. I simply use a piece of paper, write a subject in the middle of the sheet that I circle, and then I just free-associate everything that comes through, big and small, without trying to organize or put any order to my ideas. In a second step, when I feel that I have gotten all of my ideas down, I start to look for connections, regrouping ideas and discovering new ones. It's a great process to prepare for a group session on a known theme.

Exercises

The following exercises will help you dream:

- What are some of the trends that will influence your world in the years to come? List three that are connected to your dreams, three that are a threat to your dreams, and three that are neither threats nor connected to a dream but that you could take advantage of?

- What happens if you mix movement and visioning or ideation? What physical activity can you invite your colleagues to? Fishing? A calligraphy workshop? A play? It can be anything to explore movement, play, and dreaming.

- What will your organization look like in five years? Twenty-five years? One hundred years? What would your business do if it had to save the world from its most pressing challenges with the superpowers and genius it has. What would be the story?

- Identify your important responsibilities, functions, and tasks. Which of those are you certain that a robot will not be able to do in the next three to five years?

- What's the proportion of time you spend on functions that are more difficult or impossible to replace? Are you happy with that amount of time? Would you like to spend more time in that zone? What would be your plan? Apply the same reflection to your team.

- Do you mind-map or free-associate? Think of an issue where you feel stuck, somewhat paralyzed. Ex.: "My team struggles to share feedback candidly." On a blank piece of paper, in the middle, simply write what a positive outcome for that issue might be. Ex.: "My team shares more candidly their feedback with each other." In free association mode, or in mind-mapping mode, you just write down as many ideas as possible on paper, essentially brainstorming with yourself. These ideas can take many forms (solutions, people to meet, session to organize, resources to read, etc.). After you feel that you've generated enough ideas, you can start to identify the most important items that you could start to act upon.

- Identify a few places near your workplace where nature—a park, a field, a river—is present. Organize a meeting there and see what happens. Communicate in advance about your intentions, encouraging people in your team to prepare. Can you think of other unusual places to hold a usual meeting to help break the routine in a playful way?

- Invent a new ritual in your workplace. It can be as simple as IDEO's ritual around sharing tea every Wednesday at three o'clock. Create your own ritual around coffee, whisky, wine, sparkling water, or food with your team. In my first year at Cirque du Soleil, I would bring a small and silly gift after every trip. Because not everyone could travel like I did, it was a simple way to organize a ritual around sharing the benefit of traveling with the rest of my group and an opportunity when we'd organize a drawing back in Montreal to laugh for a few moments together. Most of us love to win something. Think of a need that your team has right now. Rituals can help include people and connect them—what could a simple ritual look like in your organization? Mind-map a few ideas, even if they don't seem to immediately fit, even if they feel silly, and in particular if you hear a voice say that they are dumb. Write them down anyway. Revisit the next day. See what happens.

- Cook and eat together with your team. Cooking and food seem to be enjoying a renaissance in our popular culture. One source of inspiration for connection and play is about discovering food together. Discover a new restaurant in your neighborhood together with your group. Again, as mentioned earlier, one of the most efficient practices I have discovered to care, secure safety, foster trust and play, all at once, is to learn to cook and share the meal you created together with your team. Find a chef that offers such an activity, welcome with playfulness the inevitable idiosyncrasies that will stem from organizing such an activity (allergies, food preferences, etc.).

- Write questions on a piece of paper about things that worry you, concern you, or make you anxious. Fold the paper and go to sleep with it under your pillow. Explore new ideas in the morning.

- Meditate when you can to free up space in your mind for dreams to be clearer.

- Systematically think of dreams in terms of wildest, boldest, bravest. One of my impossible-beautiful dreams is to win the tennis tournament of Wimbledon. Obviously, this will probably never happen. But creating space for this dream to just exist can open a new mental route for me to explore. For example, maybe I can't win the tournament but I could eventually practice on one of the courts and draw immense satisfaction from the experience. Or perhaps, I could play a mini tennis game on one of the practice courts against Roger Federer. I could pretend that I'm in the final and literally play with my dream. List three dreams you have that you genuinely think are absolutely impossible but beautiful. See how you could also play with them, giving them air and a chance to morph into something equally if not more beautiful than the initial ideation.

- What if, as a follow-up question to your dream articulation, you were to ask "What if . . . ?" more often than saying "no" or "not possible"?

- Practice seeing beauty around you, and when you see it, say something kind. Start by noticing three manifestations of beauty every day. It can be the handle of your kettle, the smile of your child, or the airliner that just landed. For the first sixty days, try to find only new beauty.

- Choose one impossible-beautiful dream from your reflection that you feel you could start working on over the next five weeks. What would you do next to build momentum?

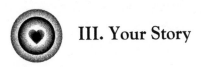 **III. Your Story**

Summary

When we are caught in the middle of the war on imagination, we lose connections with our dreams. As we progressively abandon those dreams, thinking that they are in the way of our viability and our business savvy, we start focusing on short-term goals. We hide our shortcomings under the guise of wanting to focus only on the concrete—data, analysis, and hard facts. We don't realize that we are already in the process of falling so softly that we don't know it yet. We can spend hours looking at pie chart after pie chart to convince ourselves and the world that things are as flat as our pies, but inside we probably know that this isn't so. When the war rages, we will fight against danger and limitations, padding ourselves against the first and closing our eyes not to see the second.

When we start to play with danger and limitations, something counter-intuitive happens progressively. We relax into playing; maybe we start to smile a little, or we suddenly want to win the game and go for it. And then we start dreaming. It's a space of wild ambition that's yet benevolent toward ourselves and others. It sees eyes open or closed, feels the future, and dares to answer questions that were never asked before.

This stage of dreams is essential; it represents a bridge to experiencing breakthroughs and discoveries. It's a stage of in-betweens where we are never completely sure if what we are envisioning can really happen and where we are plunged into articulating actions to come. There is also a mourning that comes from writing dreams down. As we do, there might be the feeling that we are limiting our options by stating that we want to go in a specific direction. *What if we fail? What if our dreams were the wrong ones? Will we be ridiculed, laughed at?* It might feel easier to not dream or at least to not articulate any of them and simply play it safe. But when we use play to unlock the complexity of our situation (the military uses this approach in exercises), we recognize that we have no other choice but to embrace the uncertainty of our situation. When we set impossible-beautiful dreams, we get lifted by the vitality nestled inside their mere possibility.

It would be a waste of time and energy to have small, safe, inoffensive dreams when we can have dreams that have an impossible-beautiful quality to them. We don't need to have all of our objectives under such scope, but at any given time, one of our projects or one element of our organization should be infused and riven by this idea.

Philippe Petit represents one example, and Cirque du Soleil's approach to its own limitations and the reinvention of an industry is another. Impossible-beautiful dreams stimulate real-life surprises that even their authors didn't anticipate. While more of the nondreaming parts of our work become commoditized, our clients, customers, teams, and other people we serve all ultimately look for constructive emotional responses and experiences. Therefore, we are now all in the business of moving people. Intuitively, this shows part of the road forward to sustained relevance in a fast-transforming world. Once we have the courage to dream impossibly-beautifully, we give our genius and our superpowers a new dimension and a new stage to shine collectively.

Checklist

- Is the focus on the bottom line in your organization a risk for its long-term agility?

- Who would you gather around a fishing expedition or a spa excursion to elaborate a new dream that's impossible-beautiful? If you lead the session and exploration, what would be your first three questions?

- How would you qualify your current work space when it comes to these qualities: Is there creative openness, flexibility to rearrange, formal-informal play, and collective space to connect versus solitary space to hide from the world?

- Can you post your ideas physically? Do you need to hide your idea or can you share it openly? Do you prefer one of these possibilities?

- Acclaimed visual artist Olafur Eliasson uses the expression *thinking doing* where I use *moving-dreaming*.[8] What moving-dreaming or thinking-doing activity could you invent or reinvent for your current dreaming needs?

- Where is the department of mess in your space at home and at work? If you don't have one yet, where can you start installing it? For a small area, your mess could fit in as little space as a piece of luggage offers. Based on your answer, what's your priority to improve your space if you need to?

- What if you established an eccentric collaboration with a game designer to create a custom board game inspired by your organization. Call it Challenges and Wonders. How would you brief that game designer? What would be the main question? The main challenge? What if your eccentric collaboration was to design a video game under the same theme? What if the challenges and glories of your work were reflected in a video game? What would that look like? What would you call that game? Would it be inspired by a known game or something completely new? What if you applied this thinking to a specific challenge you face at work?

CHAPTER 7

Discover Breakthroughs

The Neglected Area of Human Emotions and the Edge of the Future

Use established routines to pursue objectives, Use messiness and surprises to innovate and succeed.

Michael Carroll[1]

I. Raising the Curtain

Eventually most important breakthroughs, innovations, and discoveries are rewarded by their markets and audiences (e.g., clients, customers, employees). It's true in every sector of life. When we recognize that one innovation improves enough of our lives, we show our support by buying, subscribing, liking, and endorsing the fruit of these advances. In this way, we improve our living experiences.

I regularly think about the quality of our experiences and explore how discoveries and breakthroughs happen and how they can improve those experiences. Coming from the world of live entertainment, I primarily think about experiences and breakthroughs in terms of shows and live story experiences. Everywhere I see the potential to reveal or enhance the theatrical and emotional potential of a situation. My passion also includes a broader reflection on live experiences: from going to a theater or an exhibition, to subscribing to an online grocery service, to attending or participating in a live sports event or a rock concert, even taking a taxi.

These are just a few examples of moments and events where we will increasingly seek more constructive emotional experiences to consider them important. But this wide-ranging category of live experiences is often overlooked and neglected, even by companies whose job should be to lead research in that sector. Nonetheless, this broad sector is ripe for breakthroughs, discoveries, and innovation.

The attributes related to innovation, discovery, and breakthroughs are abundantly well documented in the business literature, if somewhat general on the most elusive elements behind creativity. Usually, we can innovate on many fronts. Roughly, we can find a way to resolve a problem that enough people will be happy to see solved and pay for its benefits. Often this will be done through leveraging technology and a business model that will generate more revenues than it needs to exist.[2] We don't find as many references on innovations and discoveries that relate to our emotional literacy, experiences, and expanding ability to connect or disconnect with others.

This area of breakthroughs and discovery doesn't fit well on a spreadsheet or a pie chart, but the question it raises remains important: How are constructive emotional reactions and experiences genuinely stimulated, triggered, and cultivated without manipulation? Taking advantage of the area of innovation typically reserved for live enter-tainment offers infinite possibilities to innovate while emotionally moving more people and, I suspect, creating more value.

Breakthrough Innovation

When I consider the nature of breakthroughs and discoveries, it almost systematically involves replacing something or making something disappear. In fact, I don't know many breakthroughs and discoveries that don't operate almost like magic. The invention of the press made the *scriptoria* (the rooms inside a monastery where monks reproduced manuscripts) and their writing monks vanish, computers made typewriters obsolete, and who knows how long we will drive our cars and buses without artificial intelligence in charge. In recent years, taxis, phones, photography, universities, and many other sectors and industries have become transformed after discoveries and break-throughs. Companies like Disney and Cirque du Soleil, for example, also triggered breakthroughs and capitalized on discoveries. Many of these innovations stemmed from old principles that continue today to inspire myriad entertainment companies and storytellers from around the world.

When I imagine creating a live entertainment experience, be it a wedding or a show in a theater, the three main aspects that my team and I try to innovate on, or to make something disappear are the *transitions* between scenes, the *separation* between the area of performance (the stage) and the audience, and the *filters* around the experience of the show (e.g., the venue, the marketing, the tactics of persuasion). The more innovation there is in those areas, the more positive the constructive emotional reactions from the audience are, which generate direct and indirect value.

When Cirque, inspired by and part of a movement of young circus troupes, reinvented the traditional circus experience in the 1980s, it brought a new theatricality to a traditional format that was essentially demonstrating acts without any attempts to create a relationship between them (transitions). From its street-performing roots, it brought intimacy under the big top by performing close to the audience, and innovated by bringing the audience onstage and by not using animals (separation). Finally, it progressively changed the context of the big top, drawing on its classic form while bringing a modern, more thematic experience to going to the circus. Cirque was also inspired by the offspring of a new movement in circus at the end of the 1960s with pioneers like the Pickle Family Circus of San Francisco and Cirque Plume in France. The big top that was mostly utilitarian (a roof and a marketing tool) became an experience, a destination in and of itself (a filter).

Constructive Emotional Reactions

Consider now emerging sectors like virtual reality and augmented reality. They too are trying to influence and break through the areas of transitions, separation, and filter. Everything about the buzzwords *immersion* and *experiences* suggests the same innovation attempts. But sectors that are not typically associated with live performance and live entertainment will continue to need constructive emotional reactions. I believe that this need will express itself in the different dimensions of our lives—as workers, clients, customers, employees, leaders—inside and outside our organizations. The organizations that will have the creative courage to leverage new technologies and innovative business models to leverage the potential behind stimulating constructive emotional reactions will bring additional disruption to our already fast-transforming world. Said differently, technology and business alone will not make the difference that considering and cultivating constructive emotional reactions will.

For example, airline carriers embrace their identity as transportation providers and industrial companies, but beyond their PR and marketing efforts, they don't often consider that customer service is part of their core business.[3] From a conventional business point of view, they innovate by solving a valuable problem (expensive fares made cheaper); using technology to cut overhead, service, and cost (self-check-in, online booking); and having a business model that innovates on old and new practices (overbooking, frequent flyer miles).

Airlines are being rewarded by markets for their breakthroughs, but I'd argue that without considering the dimension of constructive emotional reactions from their audience (their customers), they expose themselves as much as Kodak did when it forgot that its core mission and genius was to be the champion of the convenience of shared memories, not the champion of chemical paper.[4]

Breakthroughs in Live Experiences

To understand more about the potential of breakthroughs in live experiences and see how transitions, separation, and filter can calibrate our constructive emotional reactions and experiences, let's travel to Los Angeles.

I was there for work with a small group of talented colleagues from different departments of Cirque. We were all connected to the innovation and creation sectors of the company. We were being hosted by another entertainment company as part of a mission to explore the potential of a new partnership based on our respective strengths. We were to spend a few days together after hosting their team in Montreal a month earlier.

We were meeting at the Sowden House, on Franklin Avenue, between Thai Town and Los Feliz in Los Angeles. The house, designed by Frank Lloyd Wright in 1926, recalls the exotic golden age of Hollywood and a phantasmagorical interpretation of the Mayan Empire. Just arriving there was an experience to remember, but the main event was waiting for us up the long procession of stairs under our feet. It was hard to prioritize where to look, as if all that beauty around us would vanish if we didn't pay attention to it. Should we focus on the large Buddha greeting us, impassive and generous, or should we throw our laptops in the air and jump, still dressed, into the pool next to the kitchen, or settle down to observe the fish in the private pond?

We didn't have time to prioritize what to look at or what to discover. A tall man dressed like an English university professor from the 1930s, wearing tweed, a bow tie, and round horn-rimmed eyeglasses, was welcoming us, sharing the house rules and history. Scorsese's *Aviator* film had scenes here, Ellen De Generes meditated there, and dark Hollywood stories emerged too from the house's past. Staff were already busy preparing the breakfast table, and the smell of coffee, the sun, and our enthusiasm completed the sense that this was a magical morning, an inspiring way to start our creative session.

Before leaving us at the end of the tour, the man from the 1930s, clearly passionate about the house (Was he the owner?), made sure we were aware of a precious and ancient vase that was installed in the main area where we would have lunch later. We couldn't touch it or get too close to it, but we could admire it. It was a gift from a famous director (Was it Orson Welles or Cecil B. DeMille?), and we were in luck because the vase was shown only a few times a year. The way he described it to us, this vase was worth hundreds of thousands of dollars, and maybe millions. We were now in Hollywood, and our body language changed as we moved with the extreme caution of Butoh dancers anytime we were near the vase.

We had a productive and splendid morning session. Our host had showed so much care that safety was secured, and the morning had deepened the trust between our teams. We were ready to play with danger, ready to be vulnerable together and dream impossible-beautiful dreams. We broke for lunch. The kitchen staff, a team of six, stealth-dressed in black, had efficiently transformed the breakfast table into a lunch I could only label California Homage; even the salads and gorgonzola cheese rhymed with *artisan*.

I ate with delight, feeling good and enthused as discussions sparkled at our table. Then, before I saw him, I heard from the corner of my ear one of the waiters excusing himself and nervously trying to gain our attention.

He explained that he was inspired to serve us and that his dream was to work at Cirque du Soleil. He had seen every production several times. He glanced at the kitchen as if he didn't want the rest of the staff to know what he was doing as we sat there, looking at each other as we struggled to find balance between disbelief and amusement. The waiter proceeded to inform us that he wanted to offer us a live demo of his performance skills over three different pieces. He pulled out a manila envelope tucked under his black shirt and gave it to me before starting promptly to sing. He sang with all his heart, and our group, bewildered but admiring his courage, did our best to offer our sincere attention although he seemed to have focused his attention on me. At one point, one of our hosts looked at me from another table, embarrassed and mortified, and said to me what I could only read on his lips: "I'm so, so sorry." At this point, we only wanted it to end. Our waiter's voice was bad; his superpower or potential for superpower was certainly not in singing. Now he added dance to his performance, entering a sort of trance of awkward singing and dancing.

I wish I had seen it coming, that I could have prevented it somehow. His frantic movement, desperate for our validation, suddenly and violently plunged in a slow-motion nightmare. Out of nowhere, his hand hit the vase. We saw it in midair and gasped. We wanted to hold it in our hand to prevent the fall, but it was too late even as it was still floating.

I was already wondering what would happen. Would they put us all in jail, where we would wait for someone to pay a $5 million bail to release us? Some of us instantly had tears in our eyes from the shock.

Then we heard the vase hit the concrete floor, its pieces flying and disintegrating, until it stopped, and silence enveloped us. A man who seemed to be the chef came out of the kitchen as we were all taking in what had just happened. His scream asking our waiter what had happened pierced the collective silence. The waiter turned his head away from the chef, singled me out from the rest of the group, and said, pointing at me, starting apprehensively and then switching to full confidence: "It's not me! It's him!!!"

A few more incredible events happened. The waiter jumped, clothes on, into the pool, escaping from the grip of the angry chef by jumping over a too-tall-to-climb fence in front of our eyes. I don't remember when exactly it was all revealed, but we soon realized that this scene had been masterfully staged by a local troupe based in L.A. They made us a live meeting experience where multiple breakthroughs occurred on making separation, transitions, and filters almost completely disappear. The vase wasn't really priceless; they'd brought one commonly used for special effects in films and onstage, and the guide was in on the plan, but the context made us—even if we were theatrical, live entertainment professionals—believe and delight to be in the story, rather than simply witness it. We entered a dream without realizing it, and it made for a memorable, inspiring experience.

The stories of the future will take a page or two from similar experiences to create unexpected moments. Interwoven in the fabric of our lives, they will take our constructive emotional reaction spectrum into account in a novel and ground-breaking way. But I think that a broader set of experiences that I call live as in-person will also innovate, surprise, and benefit from the added value.

Another way to refer to discovering breakthroughs in this context is to think about magic. When we discover a breakthrough, we experience magic: we see something disappear. Yet constructive emotional reactions refer to *being moved*. In short, the potential for innovation that's over-looked is for *magic that moves emotions*, in addition to technology, business models, and value propositions.

Magic That Moves People

Not all magic moves. Fake magic counts only on the spectacular. Ungenerous magic and manipulative magic fizzle out of our memory after a while. And when we are asked the next time to participate, we hesitate.

What makes magic real? Real magic always moves us, as in the last point of a tennis championship we passionately followed, or when we still manage to make it on time to our kid's show after a jam-packed day at work. Real magic that moves us is ordinary and extraordinary. It operates on large and small scales. What moves people the most? Love. So to move people the most is by making them feel love, loved, seen, valued. Unfortunately, dictators know that too. What moves people always has an element that's made from love. It's the source of all resonance. I'd argue that even when we do a Google search, it works in part because we still feel the reverberation of passion, dedication, love that led to its inception.

What if love was the most advanced technology and the greatest space for breakthroughs and innovation? What if our world needed it to tackle the tough, complex, inspiring challenges ahead of us? What if the secrets of breakthroughs and discovery were to build on a foundation of love, on an operating system of love? What happens when breakthroughs and discoveries are based on cultivating the magic that moves people?

 II. Insights

Practices

The following practices might help you experience breakthroughs and discoveries.

The Metaphor of the Show

What makes a show resonate, and can that understanding help us discover new ways to cultivate breakthroughs and discoveries? The minute that we start to tell a story or imagine an experience with the intention of sharing it with others, five spaces or dimensions emerge: (1) the stage, (2) the audience, (3) the promise, (4) the space around the work, and (5) the magical space.

The Stage

The stage, the most obvious dimension of them all, is where we start to do the work: where we craft the story and imagine the show. This space evolves over time depending on the medium we will use to tell the story.

We might start at a small desk, move to a conference room with a team of collaborators, and finish in a theater supported by a team of 250 people. That space shifts in dimension, but it remains the stage. The stage can nevertheless evolve to become a book, a video experience, a live show, an opening ceremony, a business conference, or something else.

The Audience
Facing the stage is a second dimension: the space of the audience. This is where you find your customers, clients, the members of your team, the people you serve, your fans, your collaborators, and others.

The Promise
A third zone is the dimension of the promise. This is what you start to share in the work. That space is there waiting for a story to be told about the work you are doing. Some use it often in the process of creating their work, and others keep it quiet until the show is released, but that space exists virtually nonetheless, and it will eventually work as an interface to the content of your work.

In the case of a live show, this includes all the marketing, PR, and other public dimensions of what is shared about the state of the work. It includes all the work of persuasion to get the audience to buy in, to see the show or the work. It finally includes the private stories we tell ourselves about our work: *I'm encouraged today. This work really sucks. I can't see the end of it. This is badass.* These are all examples of voices that can influence the promise.

The Space around the Work
The fourth area is the space around the work. This is your first encounter with the proximity of the work—in our case, the show. This is your entrance in the lobby, but it can also be the first time you see the big top from afar and you are looking for parking. It represents the very first connection, even from a distance between the promise and a representation of that promise: the space around the work (e.g., seeing the big top from the highway after buying your ticket, localizing the book cover online after hearing an interview on the public radio). The space around the work, often in subtle, unintentional ways, gives an indication to the audience that the promise that led them into the space is either false, coherent, or incoherent. Figure 7.1 offers an overview of the landscape that the design of any experiences activates.

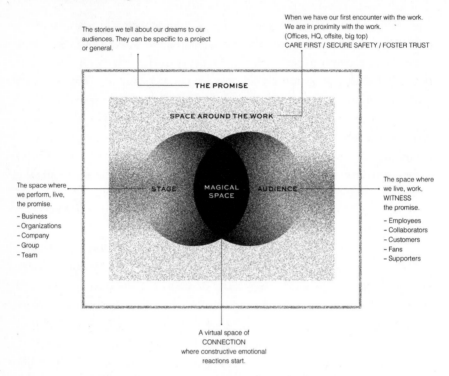

Figure 7.1   The Landscape of the Promise

The Magical Space

We normally overlook the fifth space because it is another element that doesn't fit easily in spreadsheets, financial analysis, training schedules, and other valuable operational tools. It's not anyone's fault since this dimension and "space" is invisible. You can feel it but you can't see it. However, it's the space that gives all its importance to the work onstage, magnifying its power. I call it the *magical space*. It acts like a mirror and brings, in the details of the work, something universal that the audience recognizes as its own. Usually it is a space that's left to chance, and while no one can control it, it is possible to influence it. Often, we think that we just need to put more machines and eye candy in that space to wow our audience, but that usually doesn't work very well.

We can become more intentional about offering something valuable, designing with that added dimension in mind. The magical space is a zone of resonance between the show and its audience. It's invisible yet potent, and it's usually why our experiences are memorable and relevant. The magical space is not a trick that can easily be reproduced because it's as complex as nurturing a relationship based on caring, security, and trust. Professional sports are supremely resonant and popular because their storytelling practices lead naturally to experiencing the power of the magical space. What would happen if amateur sports used some of these practices and became more aware of the magical space? I think that it would lead to innovation and breakthroughs. What if airlines and fitness clubs considered that dimension? Even if we don't create shows, what if we considered more of that dimension as well? What if we considered that space at work, with our colleagues?

Sacred Encounters

From my years at Cirque du Soleil and more generally in show business, I cherish precious lessons that I benefit from every day. One of them is that breakthroughs and discoveries are often the result of encounters— encounters between people and diverging ideas; between odd mixes that don't seem to fit at first; between artistic and sports disciplines; between the worlds of logistics, production, and staging; between pro- fessionals from all walks of life and expertise. To continue with the metaphor of the show, at the heart of all these encounters, the most fundamental one is that of the audience and of the stage. The audience represents those that you serve, inside and outside of your organizations (from your colleagues to your clients) and the stage represents your work and where the result of your work is seen, felt, noticed. Neglected or taken for granted, that relationship becomes easily commoditized, but when we consider it sacred and a life source to our work, the ultimate reason why we do what we do, then the magical space that emerges gives rise to long-lasting memories, relevance, and value.

From Live Show to Live Experiences

Discoveries and breakthroughs in a live show happen mainly through innovating on separations, transitions, and filters. Usually it's more difficult to make them seem to disappear. But it's also possible to innovate by creating surprises about how we use these techniques or about transforming what they mean or can do. From live show to live experiences, we can apply these ideas as well as some companies have started exploring them. Southwest's general boarding is one example of an attempt at transforming a transition to improve it, as is the Montreal Canadiens hockey club's use of the pregame (transition) to create a multimedia performance and added media placement. Likewise, Smart Lab in Toronto started using music and a choir to discover the effects of learning music during our senior years.

No Hard Rules but a Few Principles

Separation: The More Access through Doors, Stairs, Bridges, Ramps, Ropes, and Trapezes between the Stage and the Audience, the Better

Of course you can enjoy a live experience where none of these access points and openings exists, but to create the magical space between your audience and the work, these metaphorical doors, trapezes, ramps, and the others help make the connection a possibility. Some forms of access might be easier than others, and the circulation should be allowed in both directions. Audiences have different connection and access points to the stage, and the performers of the work also have different access points to the audience. This creates the possibility of a relationship without an easily predictable path, which creates more chances for surprises. This doesn't mean that the stage is a free-for-all, just that it is open and aware of its audience, and preoccupied not only with the work but with the impact on the audience. Holding a physical book with your hands can be a great example of reducing separation; if the author reads to you, that separation can be furthermore reduced. The trend of creating stadiums where fans see the action from seats placed closer to it is also another attempt at reducing the separation within the experience.

If the director of your organization only greets certain people on your staff but never greets clients, he or she also sends a message of enhanced separation. If your business makes it very difficult for your clients to report a problem or complaints don't get answered easily, then perhaps you have created a line of fire between you and your audience. A line of fire can be spectacular, as can be the counter of your reception desk, but both certainly discourage most people, in most cases, from jumping over to connect.

Transitions: Connecting Invitations, Welcoming, Intermission, and Saying Good-Bye

How you invite someone into your home influences the evening you will have together. Too often, the rituals around inviting guests, welcoming them into the space of your work, taking care of them, and saying thank you and good-bye to them can be disjointed and even defeat your purpose of nurturing the magical space.

Uber is a recent example of a company that tries to address some of the issues related to calling a taxi: not knowing where the cab is, not knowing if the driver will accept your credit card or if you will need to stop at an ATM, whether you will have to negotiate with the driver as to whether he will charge you for the wait, not knowing if the taxi will be clean, not knowing if the driver will give you a receipt that he writes or a blank paper that you will forget to file for your expenses later. Companies like Uber are addressing these conventional but difficult issues of transitions. Of course, if a company like Uber that promotes convenient mobility doesn't practice caring first, to secure safety and to foster trust, its goal of convenient mobility—its magical space—might be negatively affected in the future. We can choose to focus on a limited set of practices playing with limitations and danger, discover breakthroughs and grow, but history shows us that we do so at our own risk.

In other words, it will be more difficult for a company to establish a magical space with its audience (both internally and externally) if it doesn't embrace the practice of the different stages (care first, secure safety, foster trust, play with danger, dream). Notably, neglecting the first three (care first, secure safety, foster trust) makes the breakthroughs in technology, business models, and value propositions more volatile. Your inner culture always risks having unpredictable impact, positive and negative, on your innovations and how your audience perceives them.

Filters: Are You Trapped in Success? Moving Away from Common Addictions

When we experience success with our efforts, to help us cope and boost our profitability, we build an operational model that helps us scale to the level that will meet the new demand. When we grow fast or experience a long period of growth, we can develop three major addictions that prevent breakthroughs and fostering the magical space between us and our audiences.

The first is addiction to our business models, thinking that they will sustain us forever until they don't and we are caught playing catch-up. The aspirations of our audiences are not fixed, and the perception of rigidity in the way we do business suggests a rigidity in our own context. Surprisingly, expressing flexibility and therefore creativity in the evolution of our model for business can contribute to nurturing a magical space. If my milk vendor and Amazon work together to deliver the next carton of milk by drone, 24/7, right when I realize that I forgot to buy some at the store earlier, a magical space is created between the vendor and me—until that space too gets commoditized.

The second addiction is to the aesthetics, and confusing them with content. This means imitating your past successes rather than expressing something deeper, what you stand for. It's more obvious in the entertainment and related industries where the validation from audiences for one product can give the impression that you then need to create anything new with that same aesthetic. Understanding more the value of the content and why your audience celebrates it proves more sustainable and prevents you from turning your heritage into a caricature of your past success. You avoid taking your past success literally. Fashion brands directly face this challenge and represent a great example of the dilemma we face of falling into the imitation of who we are (the trap) or understanding how to express and articulate what we stand for (harder but more the trigger of the magical space) in our work.

Finally, one of the greatest conundrums that prevents us from creating a magical space with audiences is building modes of operation that make our logistical work strong but prevent faster, more flexible adaptations. As audiences' tastes and aspirations continue to evolve rapidly, magnified by the power of new technologies (e.g., more choice, better curation, easier ways to share what we like and don't like with our network), the advantages of having a strong operational model to scale our products and services makes sense, but only to the point that we can also adapt, transform, or even abandon those modes for new ones.

Audiences are asking for more intimacy, more immediacy, more proximity, and more flexibility across industries. Audiences are asking to be considered and seen. Even as we are captivated by our screens, we also scream for presence. This might explain why audiences, when they have the luxury of choice, prefer to allocate more of their spending to experiences. This calls for more flexible operational modes and goes against the concept of building operational models with a ten- to fifteen-year time span if there is no way to adapt them or transform them completely as circumstances and tastes evolve. Although the restaurant industry struggles overall, it is exceptionally well positioned to not only deliver operational excellence but also create magical spaces of connections that move people and create value. Many outliers in that industry are experiencing exceptional growth because they zag when the rest of their industry zigs.

The Best Context for Discoveries and Breakthroughs

Capture the Gifts from Accidents and Messiness

As intentional as we might want to be at cultivating magical spaces with audiences, we augment our capacity to take advantage of breakthroughs and discoveries by accepting or reminding ourselves that accidents and messiness will happen along the way. Breakthroughs count on accidents and messiness to manifest. I love that the founder of Zumba had the idea of creating what eventually became a global fitness trend after he forget his usual fitness music tape. Not having the time to go back to get it, he decided instead to break the rules and use a party music tape he had in his bag.

Cirque's founders' initial vision was to integrate animals in their shows, but once they realized how much space they needed for that, they abandoned the idea for the initial show but kept the paradigm that real circuses have animals. Eventually they discovered that not having animals was part of their unique selling proposition and understood the value of making it a prized characteristic. Similarly, after letting one of our performers go during the creation of *MJ ONE*, I had a dream that led to bringing a new artist to the show who was a sensation that we never planned for.

The list of accidents and messy situations that leads to breakthroughs is very long. When we acknowledge this wholeheartedly in our planning, another magical thing happens: we can take advantage of accidents and messiness, transforming them into advantages.

Be Patient with Deadlines

Whoever says that innovation and breakthroughs are straight lines is lying. Similarly, the worst thing for a plant is to have a team of gardeners pull on its frail leaves to accelerate its expansion. As they peer over the poor plant, they don't realize that they create a shadow, preventing photosynthesis. The plant needs light, not incessant prodding! Still, how do we know when to be patient and when to rush when cultivating breakthroughs at work? There's no simple answer since the process of discovery can never be completely dictated or ordered. Nevertheless, smart deadlines are full of virtues to create focus. When you regularly discuss those deadlines with your team, they make more sense than when they are arbitrarily imposed. In this way, you put additional pressure on your team's ability to foster trust and excel at harmonizing different sectors of your organization with conflicting priorities.

Surround Yourself with Beauty

The more we expose ourselves and our teams to beauty and share our impressions with our group, the more we improve collectively at recognizing a breakthrough and agree when something is not. Millions are lost yearly when the board's understanding of what a breakthrough is and the creative department's understanding are not aligned or harmonized. The more that beauty and benchmarks for breakthroughs are shared, the better the evaluation is of the project to focus on and develop. Obvious beauty includes visiting a museum, cycling in nature, hanging out with our kids, but also less obvious sources like the way rain might fall on your windshield or how the sound of your coffee machine in the morning reminds you of a cat purring. The point is to find your own source of beauty, big and small, from seeing a show from an artist you like to noticing the nice shoes worn by a colleague.

Trust in the Discovery Process

Part of the process that stimulates real breakthroughs involves setting ambitious goals—what I call *impossible-beautiful dreams*—that are clear, and the other part is to trust the process of discovery even as this process is hard to put in the format of key performing indicators. I prefer to use constructive emotional reactions and creative performing indicators as a sort of road map to help break down what I see as a potential list of achievements toward the anticipated objectives. This list will evolve over time, but it allows tracking the progress of broad objectives. If your breakthrough objectives don't resist being easily broken down at first into key performing indicators, it is probably not ambitious or bold enough. The connecting element between setting clear, bold intentions and breaking them down into creative performance indicators is trust. Part of the process of discovery is inevitable with intelligent patience if we are ready to be surprised by the result.

Use Free Time and Travel Time

How much time do you have to free-associate and travel to discover random things that might or might not be related to your projects? This is challenging in a low-growth economic era where organizations are cautious about investments and spending that are not directly related to an initiative, but the value of free time and of traveling can't be understated in the process of discovery. A beautiful mantra that I kept from my years at Cirque du Soleil and that I try anytime I can to apply is to stay an extra day during work travel just for the sake of provoking something unexpected and unplanned.

Commit after Dreaming

The process of working toward breakthroughs presupposes big dreaming beforehand. Despite the many merits that come with dreaming ambitiously, the process can rapidly trigger more ideas, concepts, and directions than we can handle, overwhelming us. If you work in a crazy-making or hyperactive culture where activity equates creativity, growth and success can also lead to an overabundance of initiatives. Each day, that makes it harder to distinguish what's truly important as the pile of potential projects and the priorities build up. Meanwhile, the risk is real that other, nimbler companies will take pieces of your business you might have developed, even invented.[5] After a burst of inspiration, the risk to manage is losing focus because we started too many initiatives at the same time or having a deficient process for choosing what to focus on because our collective purpose is not clear (the bottom line is the worst filter in those situation).

The biggest issue is to have a false process of evaluation of the projects to prioritize, leading to increasing cynicism.

Believe in the Importance of Diversity

I can't emphasize enough the power of diverse teams (gender, geography, age, background, discipline, outlook) to cultivate breakthroughs and discoveries in a world that's less monolithic than it was fifty years ago. The more a work culture can intelligently help people from a variety of backgrounds work exceptionally well together, the more impact it can have on the ability of the company to innovate. As a minimum, it can offer products, services, and experiences with diverse points of view harmonized inside the offering.

Draw on Your Creativity, Imagination, and Innovation

Although you need to attach teams to projects with clear innovation goals, it's tempting to tag an area, an office, or a team as creative while forgetting to forge a creative, imaginative, and innovative culture throughout your organization. Imagination and creativity shouldn't be the exclusivity of the creative department if you have one.

For a profound breakthrough to happen in your organization, the spirit of creative courage needs to evolve and eventually weave through the entire group. I owe one of my best casting discoveries to the secretary of the casting department, who hesitantly came to see me with something she'd seen in a magazine. If I didn't believe that nonexperts could propose anything to me, she might have refrained from suggesting that I look at the article about the choreographer. Being open to all ideas, no matter where they come from, is another great practice that can lead to breakthroughs.

Give Feedback to Creative Innovation Work

Whenever you are in the position of commenting on work in development, take as many notes as you need to, and then identify the three to five that are the most important, relevant, and amenable to improving the work in important ways. Share these, and let the rest sit. Often, when you address the most important notes, the work transforms, and what you thought was important is not anymore. If sharing notes where you work is highly collective and collaborative, agree beforehand on the right way to share impressions on the work. Of course, doing it with candor, what I call *real-kindness*, makes it about the work, not about the person doing the work.

Distinguish between Notoriety and Breakthroughs

If we forget the importance of working at creating breakthroughs, thinking that our models for growth are eternal or that they don't need to be reviewed regularly, we run the risk of confusing breakthrough with reputation. Bringing popular, known talent on a project doesn't mean that they are the right choices to foster breakthroughs and discoveries. Popularity, in fact, rarely replaces excellence. Getting to excellence means assembling the right talent to work on the right projects. To do that, you need to have people on your team with the superpower of creating an exceptional curation of talents.

Exercises

The following exercises will help you with breakthrough and discovery:

- The field of research at the intersection of technology, innovative business models, and constructive emotional reactions is still small. How would you start designing a live experience (as opposed to a live show) in your field with magic that would move people? If you were to design one initiative tailored to your industry, your sector, or your field, what theme or topic would you explore? Would you start on your own? Are there others in your organization or on your team who have superpowers or genius that could contribute to your reflection? What ethical principle would you add so that the research is empowering as opposed to manipulative?
- Search for the name of your organization on Google, and read what the Google page, not yours, says about who you are and what you do. Is it congruent with the story you want people to know about you?
- How would you map three to seven macrosteps or macrostages that would serve you as creative key indicators?

- Are in a crazy-making culture? Is volume celebrated as a sign of creativity? If you had to choose just one project to develop with supreme excellence over the next six to ten months, what would it be?

- How would you grade your process of evaluation to accept new projects or develop new leads? Are people inside your organization enthusiastic, cynical, indifferent, or ignorant about that evaluation process? What do you think is missing to improve that evaluation process if you have one in place? Are you the person who can lead that change? If not, who can you partner with? What would be your top three to five criteria to make the best evaluation of new projects and new leads?

- What would be game-changing in your field? What would change the paradigm of your industry? Do you have innovation initiatives related to this paradigm or project?

- Are you traveling for work over the next three to six months? How would you design your trip if you had to stay an extra day? Would you go to a museum? Dine at a famous restaurant? See the popular local sports team? Visit a center for those in need? Explore another aspect related to your industry? If you had to do something that would make your heart sing on that extra day, what would that be?

- What if you created an extra day of free time, even when you are at home? How would you design that day? What if you offered that extra day to your team, as some organizations have started to do?

 ## III. Your Story

Summary

- Innovating by discovering breakthroughs in the field of constructive emotional reactions is often overlooked, neglected, or leveraged in unethical ways.

- Beyond live shows and live entertainment, we increasingly seek and expect constructive emotional reactions from experiences covering a wider range of activities not associated to entertainment.

- Breakthroughs in entertainment cover three main areas beyond story, and they always involve making something disappear: transitions between scenes, separation between the stage and the audience, and filters around the experience of the show. Breakthroughs and discoveries in those areas improve the constructive emotional reactions from the audience.

- An example of where live experience could go in the future when you innovate on transition, separation, and filters is illustrated in the story about the vase and the server.

- Think in terms of magic and emotions what you consider breakthroughs. In any field, a new source for breakthrough and innovation could come from leveraging magic that moves, in addition to technology, business models, and value propositions.

- To make magic that moves people, five dimensions frame our work through the metaphor of the creation of a show: the stage, the audience, the promise, the space around the work, and the magical space.

- Magical space is a space of connection and the greatest trigger of magic that moves. This is a space of tremendous potential for innovation.

- Three principles can make breakthrough more concrete for live experiences:

  ○ Exchanging as opposed to demonstrating: the more doors, stairs, bridges, ramps, ropes, and trapezes between the stage and the audience, the better.

  ○ Weaving together the beats of an experience that are the invitations, the welcoming, the intermission, and saying good-bye.

  ○ Moving away from addictions to rigid operation and business models. Resist the temptation to imitate your past success to the point of becoming a caricature of what you were. Cherish the past and understand what worked, but don't dwell on it.

- The most fundamental encounter is that of your audience and your work.

- Inspiration time or unplanned time is valuable for breakthroughs. Adding an extra day to a business trip could help you see new perspectives.

- Commit after dreaming. At some point, choices need to be made and commitments articulated.

- Creativity, imagination, and innovation should characterize the entire organization rather than be constrained to a department. In start-ups and growing structures, the opportunity to cultivate this spirit rather than playing catch-up later is a compelling case to invest time in making the innovation process and mind-set open to all, even with specialists leading.

Checklist

- Do you know what success looks like when you think about what breakthrough, discovery, and innovation mean in your field?

- If resources and time were unlimited, who would you bring onto your team to define that breakthrough or help you achieve on the vision you already have?

- Think about the interactions that you have with your audience or your work. Where do you see that a deeper connection could benefit your project and have a positive influence on your innovation efforts?

- When you reflect on the deep needs and aspirations of your clients and customers, what do you think that they celebrate about you and your organization? What might they have loathed? What has left them indifferent?

- Think of the encounter between your work and your audience. How would you describe it? What could happen if you added an element of magic? What if, through this encounter, the emotional experience of your audience was enhanced, improved, magnified? What would that look and feel like, even if it doesn't make sense in the real world? What would the cultivation of the magical space add to the quality and the impact of your work?

CHAPTER

8

Grow

What If It's Not about the Logo?

Please don't fall in love with what you've constructed. It's like in the Marines—don't fall in love with your plan, because the plan's always going to change. And you need to make sure that the audience is the most important person in the room. Because if you want to make something that is memorable for somebody else, as well as for yourself—the purpose of playing, of doing live music, is that it's like a communal witnessing of something.

Yo-Yo Ma[1]

I. Raising the Curtain

Maintaining the status quo in our organizations and our businesses is increasingly more difficult to preserve, even when we are successful. The global pressures to stay relevant push most of us to innovate or risk eventually disappearing. Consequently, it makes sense that we work hard to pursue personal and collective breakthroughs because they allow us to grow, despite the perils of discovery work, the creative part of our work. Yet we can get caught in a closed, self-referential loop. Like Sisyphus, we push for innovation so that we can grow to self-preserve, so we can innovate, to grow, so we can self-preserve, and the cycle continues. This loop prevents us from making sure we circulate our ideas, that our work stays open to improvement, and that we consider its deeper, more human implications. Growing suggests that we stop and ask why we are doing what we do. What's the deeper dimension of our work, and why do our organizations ultimately exist, beyond self-preservation?

Beyond the Small Stuff

If you go to Montreal and stay in the city for a few days, you will probably visit the Mile End neighborhood. A spiritual cousin to Williamsburg, Brooklyn, the Mile End's bohemian vibe is authentic. Home to communities with origins from around the world, it's one of the best areas in town to have coffee. It's also home to a cluster of creative companies, including one of the world's premier video game companies, and a nest of artists, designers, and other professionals.

Near one of the edges of the Mile End, the Falco, a warehouse transformed into a small bistro during the week, serves delicious bowls of Japanese rice, Fair Trade slow-drip coffee, and lovely pastries at shared tables. One day I was sitting at one of the counters, next to a young woman intensely looking at her computer while taking a loud slurp of soup from time to time. She had white Apple headphones on, which might explain how she was oblivious to the intensity of her slurping.

Suddenly she started talking to the screen with a stressed tone to her voice, and it took me a few seconds to realize that she was not on her phone. She was discussing a graphic design proposition that I couldn't see because I was sitting obliquely to her. I'm not sure, but her colleague appeared to want a smaller type size, and the discussion went back and forth until they settled for a reduction of 30 percent of the font. I saw out of the corner of my eye that she looked relieved.

This conversation in fact made me realize that at times I too grow anxious about the small stuff and can lose sight of what truly matters. It was a reminder to me to keep the perspective for my team and me and to develop further my skills at seeing. Anyone can lose concentration in this way. We think that it's about enlarging the size of the logo, for example, but of course it's about something bigger. This is when I realized that numbers and words can get in the way and distract us from seeing the larger picture.

For example, what if we had less compassion and were less concerned about people's growth when we refer to them as targets to capture, staff to put on the chopping block, markets to penetrate, demographics to integrate into product pipelines? What if every time we use words like *head count*, we are leaving the heart out of the discussion? What if we end up with employees who have less heart because we explicitly use words that exclude these parts of them? What if some of the words that we use to refer to growth stand in the way of deeper, sustainable growth?

One of the greatest and most deceptive dangers for organizations caught up in the war on imagination today is to become heartless in the quest for growth. We have already seen earlier some of the symptoms encapsulated by the ravages of the war on imagination: executive arrogance; myopic, compassionless vision; an addiction to current successful business models as eternal; an inability or unwillingness to embrace true diversity; and an impatient stance on research and curiosity.

Learning to Grow without Arrogance

This is true for us individuals too. How can we grow without arrogance? And if arrogance is inevitable, how can we move beyond it? Can we shine our light with generosity rather than superiority? This is a choice that comes with advantages and disadvantages. Can we be powerful without condescension? I see a link between arrogance, light, and innovation. But first I needed to discover the land past the one where we are right all the time.

A Good Divorce?

I met Yael, who would become the mother of our daughter, Ella, and eventually my wife, in Grahamstown, South Africa, in June 2003. It was my first scouting trip in the country, and I had spent a few months preparing, connecting online and by phone with South African influencers. My main mission was to scout the National Arts Festival at Grahamstown, one of the most important cultural festivals on the African continent. I had to meet as many interesting people as possible and report back on potential talent for future Cirque projects and on the feasibility of returning later that year with our audition team.

I remember witnessing a man and a woman in Cape Town near the beach. They were homeless, wore ragged, dirty clothes, and were virtually toothless. They had clearly been clobbered by life. They limped toward the car where Yael and I were sitting, unaware of our presence, fighting over a plastic bag. The man pulled in his direction awkwardly and the woman in the couple would answer back with even more violence. It was tragic but also grotesque and comical. It was an improbable plastic tango with us as their only audience. We wondered how two people could fight like that.

About ten months later, the long-distance aspect of the relationship Yael and I had developed in South Africa ended when she moved to Montreal. We later went back to South Africa to get married near the region of the Witwatersrand Mountain range in Magalisburg.

Like many other couples, we struggled to find our footing despite our deep connection and our intentions. Too soon, we stopped caring and felt less and less safe together. Trust gave way to mistrust, and playing it safe became even more bitter than not playing together at all. By the time that our beautiful daughter arrived, our hearts were full of love for her, but we couldn't find the road to dream together. It was more important for us to be right than happy when we discussed anything. We couldn't find the imagination or the creativity to transform our conflicts into something positive. We stopped growing and made the inevitable decision to separate and eventually file for divorce. We felt that it didn't make sense for the daughter we loved so much to suffer from our acrimonious fighting.

The year that led to our decision was one of the hardest for us and for Ella. I was trying to keep my personal difficulties away from the office, thinking that it was the professional thing to do. In fact, I was making things worse for everybody.

Surviving a separation is a heartbreaking, uncertain journey for everyone involved, and the kids are the first casualty. In the process of reconciliation, with myself, Yael, and our daughter, two events led to an unexpected transformation—something akin to a breakthrough and a major innovation. Although things were still challenging, Yael and I were acting out some of the clichés of couples fighting over the nitty-gritty, even after the separation. But this quote from the actress Ellen Barkin made me stop when I read it in the *New York Times*: "I know I've said this before, but I don't think a marriage has to last forever to be successful."[2] This comment offered a completely novel idea to me and my paradigm about love, separation, and divorce.

Yael and I went through the painful disentanglement typical in divorce. Eventually I met Kat, my future fiancée. We took things slowly, eventually introducing Ella to her. By complete chance, in Old Montreal, I met the author of *The Good Divorce*, Constance Ahrons, and her husband.[3] As if she had known about the *New York Times* article I had read earlier, she told me about her book and reinforced this idea that out of something as painful as a divorce, our creativity could still aspire to build something constructive that defied the common trope of eternal discord between former lovers and life partners.

Despite my anger and arrogance over our divorce, I began to see that Yael and I didn't have to adhere to the stereotype. Our therapist had in fact suggested that with patience, "the extraordinary becomes ordinary." In our case, the extraordinary started to show up in unexpected ways. It was as if the willingness to dream of a good divorce and to escape the usual storyline liberated us from the deep war on imagination surrounding our lives.

The high note of that transformation happened a few months before I left Cirque in 2016. By then, Kat and Yael had developed a genuine kinship, showing real care and kindness to each other—something unusual that went beyond my greatest expectations. I was planning to propose to Kat during the summer and was starting to dream up ways to do that, but everything felt contrived. I didn't share my plan with anyone, not even my family.

Then a week before I planned to tell Kat's parents and mine about my intentions to propose, Yael, unprompted, sent me a text: "What are you waiting for to marry Kat? She's an absolute gem, she must stay in our family!"

When I finally proposed to Kat a month later as we were flying over a vineyard in Napa, we in fact proposed to each other simultaneously!

Growing and Awareness

A tradition in theater invites us to grow by shining a light on what scares us and what we think is impossible. The process of creating and cultivating powerful, fertile cultures of innovation at work requires such creative courage. With that special kind of courage, we use the light to see what needs care, what can benefit from more safety, what needs trust, and so on. We can recognize with more ease what we need and what we can abandon. When we can't see our responsibilities and our accountability more clearly and deny to ourselves that we can make mistakes, we affect our ability to innovate, see into the future, and grow. We risk staying stuck in an invisible collective past, letting the war on imagination run our organization, our team, and our project. But when we realize that we don't have to stay stuck, growing becomes a choice that contributes to our collective creative courage. The desire to embrace our wildest dreams becomes irresistible evidence of creativity and a celebration of the potential of our imagination. We can make separations disappear.

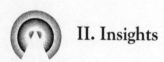 **II. Insights**

Practices

Create a Magical Space of Connection

Ironically, I grew up afraid of everyone else's talents and gifts because I figured that they had what I didn't.

In my first few years at Cirque, I was afraid that I was not enough, and I felt like a misfit. The inevitable competition at work and my colleagues' considerable talent made me feel insecure, disoriented, and doubtful of my abilities.

I eventually discovered the power of humility and compassion. I discovered that the more we offered space to others to grow, the more we grew as well. I referred earlier to the image of photosynthesis: our role as leaders is to know when to offer our attention and when to get out of the way and let everyone grow. The encounters between you and your team, other employees, and leaders offer opportunities to create a magical space of connection.

Choose Relevance over Originality

Originality is one of the offspring of creativity and imagination and is to be celebrated and cherish. It builds the foundations for breakthroughs and can be a source of great surprises. But it can replace relevance if we are seeking to create work that immediately resonates with others. Developing a talent for something unique takes time. In the circus, even when an artist-athlete trains and rehearses for two months before the opening of the show, we factor in that he or she has already been training for ten to twelve years.

Pursuing originality alone is not sustainable if it is not fueled by the search for relevance. So if I must choose between new and relevant, I always choose the latter.

Experience Layers

I believe that we can create work that considers the universal human desire to be moved. Whenever the dimension of a live experience comes into play, from the smallest event to a full-scale multimillion-dollar show, I plan and evaluate the evolution of the work through a simple set of circles, shown in Figure 8.1. Those circles represent the different layers under which you can influence separations, transitions, and filters. They also suggest that we miss an opportunity when we concentrate our efforts on only some circles. Considered together, their effect is much more powerful.

For the work to resonate, its starting point needs to be an emotional anchor in the heart of the creator or the collective heart of the team that will create the project. It means more than expressing emotions and intentions. This is where the work finds a preliminary point of view, a position, the beginning of something important to say.

The *story factor* refers to the narrative structure of the experience we have in mind. This is useful whether we use words or not to guide the audience's emotional experience. The *performance factor* refers to those

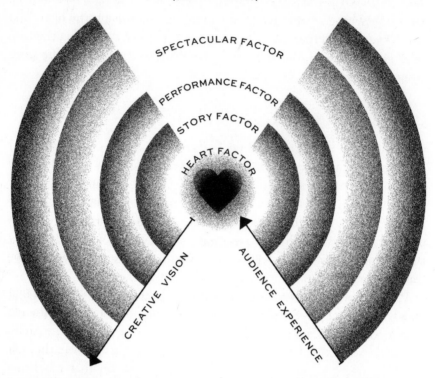

Figure 8.1   The Factors and Resonance in Live Experiences.
We tend to rely on a few of those layers to persuade and move our respective audience. My experience shows that the more we leverage all of these layers, the more our audience is moved. For the audience as well as for the ones creating for that audience, the more impactful creations start with the heart first. Another way to say that creating for the maximum impact starts with caring first.

who perform. At a hotel, for example, the staff members are part of the performance realm.[4] The *spectacular factor* refers to a panoply of effects, small and grand, that are candy for the eyes. A show created only from that circle can achieve unparalleled imagery yet fizzle in your memory as our eyes get used to anything. In the live entertainment industry, many refer to that ring also as the *wow factor*. Finally, the work that started with the heart factor adds a second heart layer over the entire project.

Figure 8.1 adds the dimensions of the creative vision and the audience experience, suggesting that the process of the work can nourish both the audience and the creators of the work. To be moved, the audience needs to have access to the work through the heart and finish the journey there. Whereas the creative team starts from the core and moves outward, the audience "enters" the experience or the work from the outside in.

Move People through Relevance

We've entered a time when it will become everyone's business to move others by offering them something memorable that's relevant to their lives. If we don't care about moving, I fear that we can be the greatest expert but our work will leave others cold. The potential for the creative relevance of your work means that the work is connected to culture. When advertising works well, that connection to culture reigns supreme without feeling manipulative.

Cirque du Soleil's humble beginnings were steeped in the culture of that time: young people were hungry to discover the world, free from the old dogma of the previous generations, and, inspired by the poetry of the circus, the call of a different life. When people entered the big top then, they felt that intuitively because it was part of a long tradition that was being reinvented.

Innovate the Right Details

During my years at Cirque du Soleil, the acrobatic team spent time developing exquisite performances in a number of disciplines. A common expression used to talk about the wow factor or the acrobatic factor was *Where's the triple?*, meaning "Where's the frisson, the shivers that you come to feel at the circus?" I think that we ask for something more subtle and powerful in the context of live performance. We are moved to see humans prevailing over unlikely circumstances, so it's less about the triple and more about the context in which we present it. We could spend a lot of time developing the quadruple or the quintuple, only to find that most of the audience missed it. That's why in figure skating, you need a commentator to raise the stakes and offer context to help the audience appreciate the nuances of the performance.

Break Your Rules but Not Your Principles

Rules are very useful and sometimes can even save lives, but they also can live forever. That's why they sometimes are used as if they are principles, which are more powerful in guiding deep thinking.

From time to time, review your current rules and see if they are all still useful. They sometimes hide paradigms that are rigid, like my ideas about what's inevitable with a divorce, that there are always animals in a "real" circus, or that athletes can't be artists.

Consider Balance versus Harmony

Before my experience at Cirque, I looked for balance everywhere, but I struggled to achieve it and I felt that I was not growing. Eventually I abandoned the idea of finding balance for the more dynamic idea of finding harmony. When I think of trapeze artists, hand-balancing artists, and Philippe Petit on a high wire, their movements suggest to me less the balance of static forces in a perfect line and more the harmony of music. Like music, they use every note, even dissonant ones. When you see a balancing act up close, you see how much movement and constant readjustment there are.

When we think about the growth of our organization, the idea of striving for harmony rather than balance is inspiring. Balance to me suggests an immovable, fixed state, whereas harmony suggests something dynamic that keeps changing, using as much dissonance as clarity.

Understand the Differences between Growing and Winning

Winning suggests an end, whereas growing is a continuous process. Creativity, imagination, and innovation also suggest a process where things are not as clear-cut and continue to evolve. When you grow collectively after you have seriously considered your audience, they also win. They benefit from the excellence of your team and your organization.

Stand for Something

Audiences need to know that we stand for something real. Our work needs to say something and have a point of view on the world. If we compromise on what we stand for and believe, they will sense it and disengage. What moves you deeply? What does your organization deeply stand for, and how do you live that message?

Transcend Your Signature and Let the Work Talk

When we let go of our grip on the result of our work and focus on those around us who will benefit from it, we realize that however personal our work is, it's ultimately not about us. As we see that the results of our work can transcend us, we take things less personally when tension arises or we feel that our work is not justly recognized. In the same spirit, I advocate letting the work talk for itself.

Love in Technology and Growth

Is it too much to refer to love in the context of work, innovation, and creativity? If creativity uses everything, if imagination is sourced through all doors, why would we leave love aside when we develop innovative projects or want to transform our work? Sometimes integrating this idea is just good design. Facebook, for example, made a small step in that direction when it evolved beyond the famous feedback platform button Like by developing Love, Sad, Angry, Haha, and Wow buttons.

Technology can evolve to reflect our need for constructive emotional reaction. BBC *Pop Up*, a TV documentary show that crowd-sources the story ideas of its audience, is another good example of an organization exploring the potential of the magical space to create with its audience.

The United Nations (UN) and world leaders have set an ambitious list of goals designed to eliminate extreme poverty in the world by 2030 with the project Sustainable Development Goals.[5] It has seventeen goals:

1. No poverty
2. Zero hunger
3. Good health and well-being
4. Quality education

5. Gender equality

6. Clean water and sanitation

7. Affordable and clean energy

8. Decent work and economic growth

9. Industry, innovation, and infrastructure

10. Reduced inequalities

11. Sustainable cities and communities

12. Responsible consumption and production

13. Climate action

14. Life below water

15. Life on land

16. Peace, justice, and strong institutions

17. Partnerships for the goals

This list both points to a full program of potential innovations and breakthroughs from now until 2030, and has the quality of wild, impossible-beautiful dreams at the foundation of deep innovation and deep growth. Still, I find that one goal is missing: "50 percent more love and beauty everywhere in the world." That would also be 50 percent more space for our innovation to promote connections, the source of real growth.

Exercises

The following exercises lead to growth:

- List two people you could help grow by offering them interesting new challenges related to their superpowers or genius.
- When you consider the layers of the experience graph and the encounters that exist between your organization and its audience, the people you all serve collectively, can you break down the experience by circles? Can you list the most important activities that you and your colleagues need to be aware of for each circle?

- List three to five of the most important guiding principles for you at work and for your organization. These are North Star types of principles like "Always partner with a company that we will have fun with" or "We always want to have one objective related to ending extreme poverty in the world."

- List three to five of your most important, almost sacred rules that have helped you succeed and do good over the last three years. When you place your list of rules next to your list of principles, do some of your rules need to be abandoned or challenged?

- If you had to develop one innovation initiative related to your work that's connected to one of the goals set by the UN and world leaders, what would the initiative be? How does it connect to your principles? Does it elicit new ones? Does it elicit new rules?

- How would you formulate the early stages of a project that would link your business and innovation goals to the initiatives you listed? List a few of the next steps. Who would you talk to next to give this project steam? Are you the best person to develop it, or do you know someone who is? If not, who could help you find the right person?

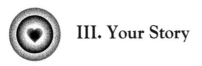 **III. Your Story**

Summary

Details are supremely important, but they can prevent us from seeing a more important picture. Developing that awareness when we are going full speed with our work can help us grow meaningfully. This practice of bringing even the most challenging problems under the light of our collective awareness is at the heart of working with creative courage. Ultimately, creative courage represents the willingness to transform our conditions and grow meaningfully.

Live experiences that we can host move us and our audiences, inside and outside our organizations.

The UN and world leaders have established seventeen goals that point to profound innovation and growth with the goal of ending poverty by 2030. What if we added another goal? What if the boldest innovation was finding new and compelling answers to the following questions:

- How do we move the people we serve and the ones we work with?
- What if the most important question to help find new solutions to our greatest challenges and greatest opportunities to innovate was to ask how love grows? In our communities, our workplace, in the heart of our drive to innovate and to orchestrate breakthroughs?
- What if technology and business models partnered in that quest? I think that love is the most ancient yet mysterious technology, perhaps the most advanced operating system. It's also the unifying factor to move people and move far away from the war on imagination.
- What if the most advanced field for our innovation dreams was the field of love?
- And what if answering that unusual call was meeting exactly what our clients, employees, customers, and audiences value the most?

We Can Be Genius, Leader, and Novice All at Once

Ultimately, I see our practice of creative courage grow—whether individually or for our organizations—through something akin to an ever-evolving wave that can grow stronger, recede, expand, or wane completely. You can use the visual tool shown in Figure 8.2 on page 160 to do a general scan of your practice at the individual, team, or wide organizational level to get a general and intuitive assessment of the potential to improve your output related to innovation and creativity toward constructive transformation. This intuitive scan can help you prioritize where to act first if some of your practices are already very strong and anchored in your culture. As its name suggests, though, starting with caring first is often the priority of priorities

In any case, I believe that just bringing more awareness to the state of proficiency and mastery you and your organization have for each dimension or practice can help bring clarity on what to do next and have the best payoff.

1. Where do I/we stand when it comes to caring first? Intuitively, and considering the nuances explored in Chapter 2, are we genius ("this is a core practice and value that I/we live by day in and day out, no matter the challenges")? Are we leader, meaning already integrating several best practices but wanting to go further, missing something, having to struggle with incidences of inconsistency, irregularity, and dissatisfaction? Or are we novice, either because we genuinely haven't spent that much time considering the dimension of caring first in our work or because for a few reasons, we are poor performers in that area, with several examples of failures to refer to. Write, from intuition, where you feel you are now. Genius? Leader? Novice? Obviously, there are no right or wrong answers, just real ones.

2. Where do I/we see the level of the dimension of securing safety? Do we consider that we are genius? Leader? Novice?

3. How about the state of fostering trust? Again, do we assess our individual or organizational culture as genius? Leader? Novice?

4. When we play with danger and limitations, are we genius? Leader? Novice?

5. Are we genius dreamers? Or leader, or novice?

6. Considering our explorations about discovering breakthroughs, are we genius, leader, novice?

7. Finally, when we put it all together and evaluate how we grow, where are we? Genius, leader, novice?

Paradoxes can abound here without considering that this is a tool that simplifies a much more complex reality—a culture can excel in discovering breakthroughs without growing; the recent, easy, chief example is Kodak, referred to previously. Or, an organization can grow without caring first or securing safety among its culture, but then the question is: For how long? How long, before its toxic culture starts to reflect on the end user? Obviously, schematics and intuition alone can't apprehend the rich and complex textures or our reality. But simplifying things, as I suggest here, can assist in breaking the cycle of confusion and can help stop in its tracks the effects of the war on imagination. A war that prevents us from seeing that we can affect positively, that handicaps our ways to lead, poisoning our lives and our organizations. In some simple ways, integrating and living through these dimensions and practices is a way to show love to our teams, our organizations, and ourselves.

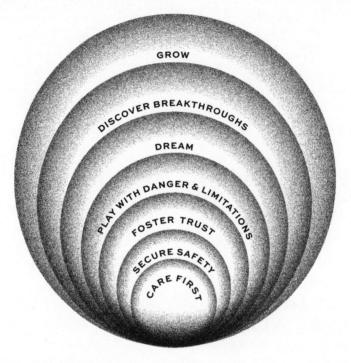

CARE FIRST: _____

SECURE SAFETY: _____

FOSTER TRUST: _____

PLAY WITH DANGER & LIMITATIONS: _____

DREAM: _____

DISCOVER BREAKTHROUGHS: _____

GROW: _____

Figure 8.2   The Framework of Creative Courage: Seven Dimensions for Innovation

Checklist

- It can feel provocative, confusing, and even inappropriate to think of love in the context of our businesses, organizations, and personal work. Seen differently, caring first, securing safety, and fostering trust are forms of real love in action that can be implemented and improved in any group. What area of your organization could benefit the most from nurturing more love as a tool for change and innovation? Can you think of a few concrete ways, inspired by your reflections in the chapter exercises, that would help support this objective of transformation, evolution, and change? Typically, growth through innovation increasingly leads to unknown, diverse information, competing realities, and challenging views.

- Who do you love, appreciate, or care for who could benefit from your initiative to create more space for them to surprise you? Can you imagine adopting a similar approach with a group that you lead so that they can impress or surprise you because of the space you create for them to do so?

- What scares you the most about the future of your work and your organization? What are the most complex, challenging problems your group currently faces?

- What would happen if you reframed one of those problems with love in mind, that is, by adding value to the human connection and human experience embedded in the problem? For example, "Our ticket sales are eroding" could be replaced by "What would we need in the next two years to enchant the people we serve?" "Despite our success, our culture is increasingly obsessed with the bottom line" can be transformed by asking "How would we go about putting a premium on people learning from each other on our team and forging deeper connections, in addition to being rigorous financially?"

- Growing often involves letting go of details that are no longer important. We face an increasing volume of information that makes it harder every day to distinguish what matters from what is merely a superfluous cosmetic. For example, even if we know that branding is about more than logos, website upgrades, and tactics (it's about the expression, superficial and profound, of the purpose an organization holds at its core), it's easier to focus on the cosmetics and hope for the best. Do you have on your project list an item that could benefit from digging deeper into your real purpose or the purpose of your organization?

- When you review the objectives of the projects you are currently working on, which projects could benefit from your transcending your signature? In other words, which projects are more about you and your organization and less about the people who might benefit from your actions and strategies? How can you make one of those projects more about the people who will benefit from it?

CHAPTER 9

Start to Dance

When Is It Too Late?

Dance, dance, otherwise we are lost.

Pina Bausch[1]

I. Raising the Curtain

My parents arrived at Las Vegas's McCarran International Airport on time, with my sister, Annie, leading the way. While they'd seen some of the big top Cirque du Soleil shows in Montreal, it was the first time that my parents had set foot in Las Vegas, Nevada, the first time they would see the result of my work as creative director, and the first time they'd spend a few days in a row in my work space. I couldn't recall if we'd ever experienced anything close to a real vacation together before, but this certainly felt the closest to such an experience. The only ones missing were my brother, and my daughter, Ella, who was in India with her mom.

My parents had worked hard all their adult lives, taking little or no vacation time over the decades, so the prospect of spending a few days together around the premiere of the MJ ONE show brought mixed feelings. Our lack of intimacy and trust meant that we don't excel at simply being together. This lack of connection made my anxiety palpable, even as it was compounded with pride and warm-heartedness for them to finally be in town, and I wanted to treat them well. I made sure their hotel room was exquisite and located as close as possible to the theater so that walking to the premiere at the Mandalay Bay was easy and that I wouldn't get last minute calls about them being lost. As I helped the driver take charge of their luggage in the airport car, I did my best to hide those feelings.

The day of the premiere brought its unsurprising swarm of activities. I had to give interviews, discuss the schedule following the premiere with our production manager (Spike Lee, Justin Bieber, and Michael Jackson's kids had confirmed for the gala premiere three weeks later), shop for a dress shirt, make sure with Kat that my family had a good place for breakfast and options for things to do, and I had to stay as calm as possible. The entire cast, crew, and creative team wanted to present a show ready on day one, and we thought that we had the potential to offer it that night.

It was heartwarming to see my parents walk along the crowded red carpet, elegant but unfamiliar with the scene, eventually finding the seats where we would all sit together. It was hard not to give context to everything that was going on around them. Should I tell them what the images on the video wall mean? Should I explain to them how I worked with these artists? Should I tell the story of the show? But it would have been somewhat abstract for them, so I just let them enjoy the experience of the show.

I stayed on the edge of my seat for the whole evening, hoping that the opening performance would be flawless. As the finale progressed, people stood up from their seats, clapping, dancing, feeling the music, and genuinely enjoying themselves. When the performance ended and the curtain fell, the audience exploded with more applause and loud cheers, refusing to leave.

After about eighteen months of work, countless days and nights working over fifteen hours straight in the theater, we, our team, had pulled it off with grace, playfulness, agility, and courage. Seeing and feeling an audience react so spontaneously, with such force and enthusiasm, to the result of our work and that of a remarkable team like the one we had was something exceptional and unforgettable. But the glory of the moment hardly registered with me.

During the show, I had barely glanced at my parents or my sister to see if they were enjoying themselves. I didn't want to look as if I were begging for compliments or encouragement. They are in fact usually unimpressed or undemonstrative, and as if I had forgotten that detail when I invited them, fear and anger started rushing through me. I decided that it had been a bad idea to have invited them all the way to Las Vegas, that it was the worst time for me to try to move past the war on imagination. *Why am I still trying to save this family?* I thought. Why was I shooting once more for world peace? I had always ended up deeply disappointed. Kat was sitting next to me and the rest of the family next to her so I couldn't see them directly anyway.

About seven minutes after the show's finale, amazed by the audience's reaction but not wanting to influence the people around me, I stay glued to my chair, as progressively, the full house of 1,805 audience members stood. I might have been the last to stand about two minutes from the closing of the curtain. By then, there was a party in the theater. I still didn't want to look at my parents, but Kat pulled my arm, looked at me, and just said: "*Look!*" My father was dancing next to my mom, immersed in the show's spirit, music, and experience. He was dancing and he was cheering. I had never seen him dance before.

The next day, we did one of the most stereotypical yet magical activities in Las Vegas: I invited the entire family for a brunch of wonder at the classic restaurant Picasso, and we had the best table in the house, facing the Bellagio fountains. I was doing it all for my parents, because I knew that this is not something they would ever do on their own. We were enjoying the warm weather under our umbrella, when my mother took me aside, as if she wanted to confide to me an interesting secret: she wanted to let me know that her sleep was interrupted several times during the night. I had wanted things to be as close to perfect for them as possible, so I worried that my instructions to the hotel didn't go through when I ask for the quietest room away from the party hotel rooms typical in Las Vegas. But she assured me that I didn't need to worry: it wasn't the reason for her interrupted sleep. She explained that several times during the night, my dad woke her up through his movement and agitation. The second time she was interrupted, she realized what was happening: in his dreams, my dad was still dancing and humming small bits of the music of the show.

If it was an improbable scenario for a kid like me who had gone from small town imitations of Michael Jackson in the East End of Montreal to lead the creation of a Cirque du Soleil hit show about Michael Jackson in Las Vegas. It was not even an impossible-beautiful dream to see my dad dance like that. It had caught me entirely off guard.

 II. Insights

Practices

It's part of the power and beauty behind living our lives with creative courage that often catches us off guard, surprises us, and ultimately rewards us because we are willing to open ourselves to the process. By welcoming more imagination and creativity into our lives or simply by applying our creativity and imagination at the heart of our lives, we open the gates of the unexpected—not only for our work and our organization but for our own lives and dreams. When we have the courage to dance with the unknown, the unknown will surprise us, and usually this makes us grow.

I can't promise that every dad reluctant to dance will suddenly change course and moonwalk, but I promise that if you try, debate about, and test just a few of the ideas discussed in this book, you will open or reopen gates that are waiting for your voice and your heart.

I think that love has a technological dimension. It's a technology that can help us relate to each other and to the rest of the world and can be improved.

I realize now that the same cycle of stages discussed in this book was also at play. It began by creating a context where I had to care first and secure enough safety for my parents to agree to come to Las Vegas and enjoy their visit. Then, slowly but surely, by fostering trust and having my dad play with danger and limitations, confined in that theater and confronting the music that he disapproved of when I was growing up, he eventually experienced a breakthrough so profound that he was still feeling its impact in his dream.

We all grew from the experience. It didn't transform everything, of course, but this was the definitive moment where we left the land of the war on imagination, embracing instead a space more open to laughter and warmth. If you don't believe in miracles through this process of awareness, you can have miracles believe in you. In various contexts, we often talk about reparation for past violence or past abuse that we have buried in the sand of our personal history, but I always wonder if reconciliation is not a more powerful aspiration. Maybe reconciliation can be an expression, an interface embedded inside the technology of love, waiting for our creative courage to innovate and imagine a constructive future.

* * *

This book has mainly looked at practicing creative courage in the context of individual and collective work. The added benefit from working with creative courage is that it can give us the mettle to declutter some of the weight that we don't need to carry. And as we become lighter, we free up space and discover a more creative, generous outlook in our personal lives.

Exercises

- Could an aspect of your personal life benefit from decluttering? Is reconciliation an option that can play an innovative role in your life? If so, how would you go about connecting the dots of the different stages?

- Is there a relationship in your life that you could safely, without risk to you or the other person, bring to some reconciliation if you were to use the principle behind creative courage? Can you recognize any voice in you that says: *It's impossible to reconcile with this person or with this situation?* If so, ask yourself why and how it's true, and once you have listed your reasons, wait a day or two. When you go back to the list, ask yourself: *Is that true?*

- If you took notes and had insights along the way, is there anyone around you who would benefit from them as well? Why not share with them by caring first!

- How could you use the different stages of creative courage in this book to design your own live experience or live encounter? A dinner? A presentation at work? Your next show at the Armory in New York?

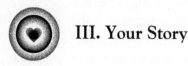 **III. Your Story**

Summary

It's never too late to start dancing after all. With the right conditions, dance can even end the war on imagination.

Checklist

- Use your impossible-beautiful dream hat. What would happen if your workplace was 50 percent more loving, benevolent, empowering, imaginative? What would it feel like and look like? Go into the details of what you and your team would need to change, maintain, or abandon. What would happen if your workplace was 50 percent more creatively courageous? Why not mind-map your ideas or create visual inspiration boards with the theme that speaks the most to you from your exploration?

CONCLUSION: 50 PERCENT MORE

Remember: *there is a life, before, during, and after Cirque*. This was the mantra that I shared with artists, performers, and athletes the world over. I made sure that I repeated the message when I was calling one of them to announce the good news that he or she (or they) was selected to run away and join our circus on one of the shows. What I was trying to convey to them is how, even though it was their dream come true to work at Cirque du Soleil, they didn't need to get gobbled up by the dream. Instead, they needed to find a way to ride the dream and continue to grow as an artist and human being, at Cirque du Soleil and beyond.

Over the years, it has been one of my greatest privileges to see artists and creators I cast in different shows or who had been cast by colleagues continue to do just that: grow and share their extraordinary talents, their superpowers, and genius in a variety of ways with the world.

I'm equally privileged and grateful to have lived, experienced, and learned so much myself at Cirque du Soleil. I learned how much diversity in all its forms matters, not only onstage but in the boardroom, at the highest level. Influence goes a long way over control, and in my thinking on leadership, I believe that we still have much more to learn about leveraging influence in a positive way. Finally, the more I actively provide opportunities for people around me to grow, the more *I* grow, even if that means that I'm helping someone who will eventually replace me.

We hear about companies that fall under the dictates of the war on imagination. The destructive cycle of that war is familiar to us. Usually it starts by not caring, then by glorifying danger and risk without having secured safety, which engenders mistrust. From mistrust, the war escalates, and we find ourselves playing it safe as our default position and in every project. It's a no-win situation where instead of dreaming, we can only think in the here and now about the bottom-line. The mental and collective space for imagination is gone. The only way then to realize breakthroughs and discovery is by turning the bottom line upside down and gaming our own system. We thought we were destined to grow but end up shrinking or cheating. And even when the situation is not extreme enough for the media to make the story public, we hear about workplaces or work in places that are increasingly heartless. Independent of financial success or economic uncertainty, these workplaces grow soulless and eventually lose credibility inside their walls and with those they serve outside.

I didn't attempt to draw a general theory of everything in this book. Instead, I have shared my personal take as a creative leader on the potential of nurturing our cultures at work comprehensively. My approach doesn't pretend to be universal or exclusive; it is based on my experience. Because the need for innovation at work will continue to grow, I believe in the value of discussing the quality of our workplaces from many points of view. In addition, the thirst for our audiences to be moved, primarily our team and the people our work serves, will also continue to grow.

I saw a distinctive value in sharing my practical reflection around the potential of workplaces to be more creative and innovative from a standpoint that was not purely about business or management. My views on practicing creative courage aim not only at nourishing our bank accounts by resonating more with our audiences; they are also intended to sustain our heart and soul. I believe that we can create and maintain organizations that not only operate and innovate at the highest level but also provide constructive, inspiring, and empowering space for their employees, teams, and collaborators to grow. This should be the subject of many discussions and many prototypes, but I suspect that there will never be one solution that works for everyone. Therefore, I have proposed a framework that you can tweak, adapt, and, more important, test-drive to improve with your reality in mind.

I hope that the discussions and the debates about making our workplaces more creative and more skilled at innovating collectively are only starting. It's a topic that will benefit from exchanges between many voices: old and new, young and old, CEOs and entry-level employees, chief information officers and art directors, experts and practitioners, human resources leaders and music leaders—diverse voices in every possible shade and degree.

We saw that these stages and this framework can operate inside-out and outside-in for us. We can use the framework with our team to help us both scan our organization and also create a deeper connection with our audience or the people we serve.

1. *Care first.* Creative courage is not elitist. There is a tremendous potential in discovering, understanding, and celebrating our aspirations, superpowers, and genius. We can all take the path toward discovering these past the clichés. It doesn't start with respect; it starts with care.

2. *Secure safety.* Although the secret peace negotiations in Oslo in the early 1990s ultimately failed, when asked, the initiator, Mona Juul, and her husband, Terje Rød-Larsen, from Norway, stressed how important it was to secure safety among the members of the negotiating team. Setting a positive and concrete context where everyone can see the net prepares the team for trust.

3. *Foster trust.* This is where collaboration can be built inside and outside organizations. The stronger that care and safety are, the better is the chance of fostering trust.

4. *Play with danger.* Limitations and danger are inevitable when we are trying to innovate. But if we decide to play and transform them into advantages or attributes of our innovation, unexpected things happen. Without much trust, safety, and care, you are less likely to jump and try to execute a new back flip wholeheartedly.

5. *Dream.* Dreams don't make literal sense for a reason: they are designed to be impossible-beautiful and to set our work on an even more ambitious path that we could have envisaged. Setting ambitious financial goals is completely legitimate but doesn't qualify in the impossible-beautiful category. Great financial returns are the result of well-executed impossible-beautiful projects.

6. *Discover breakthroughs.* Conventional innovation, which roughly points to what we already know, is still relevant today and leverages technology, business models, and value propositions. In discovering breakthroughs, we identify the growing need for constructive emotional reactions or experiences. Audiences, both inside and outside of organizations, have an opportunity to bring valuable and distinctive solutions that also take that dimension into consideration. We can all

play a role in cultivating these constructive emotions that favor moving beyond transactional connection toward emotional connections.

7. *Grow.* If we let the details eat our lives, we miss the possibility for deeper transformation. How could we leverage in our aspirations one of the seventeen goals set by the United Nations and our world leaders? What if we added an eighteenth goal, "By 2030, 50 percent more love and beauty, everywhere in the world"?

Then we can start over, from anywhere in the framework, and focus on the stage where we think we need to offer our attention. For as long as we understand the sequential and incremental nature of each stage in relationship to each other, we can also review our individual work with the same tool and identify areas to celebrate and areas to develop further.

As a creative professional, an artist, a manager passionate about leading people with as much humanity as possible, I often wondered if we had to make a choice between excellence and benevolence, between light and arrogance. I discovered that the answer is not that simple because it is a choice that we make: to join the secret society of creative courage rather than the dark side of the Force.

I can't claim any scientific causality between added care or added trust in the workplace and higher market share prices or a greater innovation potential. I can only share two things on that point. First, between light and arrogance, you can always choose light, even when you have chosen arrogance a thousand times before. In other words, light is always accessible. Second, workplaces that become serious about improving their collective and individual creative courage will not only have a great impact on the world but a positive one on their teams as well. Creative courage is a mind-set and a set of practices accessible to all of us. The world is waiting to be moved by you.

NOTES

Introduction

1. Quoted in Thomas L. Friedman, "From Hands to Heads to Hearts," *New York Times*, January 7, 2017.

Chapter 1

1. Yumi Sakugawa, *Your Illustrated Guide to Becoming One with the Universe* (Avon, MA: Adams Media, 2014).
2. Jessica Shepard, "Fertile Minds Needs Feeding," *Guardian*, February 10, 2009.
3. Tom Kelley and David Kelley, *Creative Confidence: Unleashing the Creative Potential within Us All* (New York: Crown, 2013).

Chapter 2

1. Simone Pétrement, *Simone Weil: A Life* (New York: Pantheon Books, 1976, p. 462).
2. Euronews, "Hollande Urges 'Respect' in Bid to Calm Paris Suburb Violence," Last Update, February 14, 2017, http://www.euronews.com/2017/02/14/hollande-urges-respect-in-bid-to-calm-paris-suburb-violence.
3. "Orange-Owner France Telecom to Act after 23 Suicides by Staff," *Telegraph*, May 6, 2017, http://www.telegraph.co.uk/finance/newsbysector/mediatechnologyandtelecoms/telecoms/6189984/Orange-owner-France-Telecom-to-act-after-23-suicides-by-staff.html; Aimee Swartz, "Workplace Suicides Are on the Rise," *Atlantic*, March 17, 2015,

https://www.theatlantic.com/health/archive/2015/03/workplace-suicides-are-on-the-rise/387916/.

4. Renée Mauborgne and W. Chan Kim, "Blue Ocean Strategy," *Harvard Business Review*, October, 2004, https://hbr.org/2004/10/blue-ocean-strategy.

5. Gay Hendricks, *The Big Leap: Conquer Your Hidden Fear and Take Life to the Next Level* (New York: HarperCollins, 2009).

6. Elizabeth Gilbert, *Big Magic: Creative Living beyond Fear* (New York: Riverhead Books, 2015).

Chapter 3

1. https://www.brainyquote.com/quotes/quotes/m/milesdavis130826.html

2. "O" is a Cirque du Soleil show created in 1998 and presented ever since at the Bellagio Hotel in Las Vegas.

Chapter 4

1. Carlos Baker, ed., *Ernest Hemingway: Selected Letters 1917–1961* (New York: Charles Scribner, 1981).

2. Ron Heifetz and Martin Linsky, *Leadership on the Line: Staying Alive through the Dangers of Leading* (Boston: Harvard Business Review Press, 2002).

3. Eventually the casting advising team grew beautifully under a different context and leadership. Despite the hardship, I kept my eyes on some of the precious lessons from that time.

Chapter 5

1. Lucas Dietrich, 60: *Innovators Shaping Our Creative Future* (London: Thames & Hudson, 2009).

2. Trampo-wall parks have opened around the world since then. *La Nouba* was the Cirque du Soleil show where it was first featured in 1998 at the Walt Disney World Resort in Orlando, Florida.

3. E-180 is a Montreal-based company with events around the world that promote finding "like-minded people interested in sharing knowledge

face-to-face, one-on-one." The events are often set in a playful, relaxed environment. (https://static.e-180.com/about/whoweare)

4. Hackathon has a sprint-like format that creates a concentrated moment in time and assembles a multitude of resources and talent into one room. Typically, a few challenges are launched all at once, mixing creative, technological, and industry-specific elements to solve.

5. The famous Design Thinking course at Stanford University offers a great introduction online, Virtual Crash Course in Design Thinking (https://dschool.stanford.edu/resources-collections/a-virtual-crash-course-in-design-thinking).

6. Verity Studio, based in Switzerland, is composed of "a team of entrepreneurs, engineers, artists, live events professionals, mathematicians, and designers who believe that drones will fundamentally transform the live events experience." (http://veritystudios.com/about-us/)

7. Jamie King has directed and led the creative direction of some of the highest-grossing rock and pop concerts of the past two decades. He's been a close collaborator and creative director for Madonna, Bruno Mars, Michael Jackson, and Prince, among others.

8. Hanna Rossin, "The Overprotected Kid," *Atlantic Monthly*, April 2014, https://www.theatlantic.com/magazine/archive/2014/04/hey-parents-leave-those-kids-alone/358631/.

Chapter 6

1. Philippe Petit, *Creativity: The Perfect Crime* (New York: Riverhead Books, 2014).

2. The documentary *Man on Wire* won an Academy Award in 2008.

3. Michael Chui, James Manyika, and Mehdi Miremadi, "Where Machines Could Replace Humans—and Where They Can't (Yet)," *McKinsey Quarterly*, July 2016.

4. This is my hypothesis: we might be moving from conventional brand symbols to complex, overt feeling signatures that we associate with for a while and that might evolve with us. Companies of the future might have feeling signature portfolios rather than brand portfolios.

5. Paul Auster, *Why Write?* (Providence, RI: Burning Deck, 1996); Elizabeth Gilbert, *Big Magic* (New York: Riverhead Books, 2015).

6. Desk toys that promote thinking with our hands and subtle free associations of ideas, https://www.ludusludi.com/.

7. David Allen, *Getting Things Done: The Art of Stress-Free Productivity* (New York: Penguin Books, 2001).

   On the importance of developing free-association skills (so called daydreaming abilities) as promoted by mind mapping. "Children are trained to think linearly instead of imaginatively; they are taught to read slowly and carefully, and are discouraged from daydreaming. They are trained to reduce the use and capacity of their brain." Tony Buzan (https://www.brainyquote.com/quotes/quotes/t/tonybuzan676114.html).

8. Marina Abramovic, ed., *Akademie X: Lessons in Art + Life* (New York: Phaidon Press, 2015).

Chapter 7

1. Michael Carroll, *Awake at Work: 35 Practical Buddhist Principles for Discovering Clarity and Balance in the Midst of Work's Chaos* (Boulder, CO: Shambhala Publications, 2004).

2. Marc de Jong, Nathan Marston, and Erik Roth, "The Eight Essentials of Innovation", *McKinsey Quarterly*, April 2015.

3. Scott Anthony, "Kodak's Downfall Wasn't About Technology," *Harvard Business Review*, July 15, 2016, https://hbr.org/2016/07/kodaks-downfall-wasnt-about-technology.

4. Farhad Manjoo, "How Technology Has Failed to Improve Your Airline Experience," *New York Times*, April 12, 2017.

5. As an example, could Cirque du Soleil have capitalized on the trampo-wall nascent industry and become its leader, having originated the concept? Sky Zone's revenues in 2016 were $240 million according to CNBC's Jane Wells. Sky Zone is the current leader in the category of trampoline parks.

   Jane Wells, "This 31-Year-Old CEO Is Making Millions from Trampolines," *Make It*, CNBC, June 8, 2016, http://www.cnbc.com/2016/06/06/this-31-year-old-ceo-is-making-a-fortune-off-trampoline-idea.html.

Chapter 8

1. Yo-Yo Ma speaking to Krista Tippett, "Music Happens between the Notes," *On Being*, NPR, September 4, 2014, https://onbeing.org/programs/yo-yo-ma-music-happens-notes/.
2. Alex Witchel, "Ellen Barkin Is No Uptown Girl," *New York Times*, April 22, 2011.
3. Constance Ahrons, *The Good Divorce* (New York: HarperCollins, 2009).
4. B. Joseph Pine II and James H. Gilmore, *The Experience Economy* (Boston: Harvard Business School Press, 2011).
5. United Nations Development Goals: http://www.undp.org/content/undp/en/home/sustainable-development-goals.html.

Chapter 9

1. *Pina*, directed by Wim Wenders. (2011; Berlin, Germany: Neue Road Movies, 2013), DVD.

INDEX